OPPOSING VIEWPOINTS® SERIES

WITHDRAWN

America's Great Divide

Other Books of Related Interest

Opposing Viewpoints Series
Party Politics
Government Gridlock
Trumpism and the Future of the Republican Party

At Issue Series
Partisanship
The Politicization of the Supreme Court
The Media's Influence on Society

Current Controversies Series
Libertarians, Socialists, and Other Third Parties
Nativism, Nationalism, and Patriotism
The Capitol Riot: Fragile Democracy

> "Congress shall make no law ... abridging the freedom of speech, or of the press."
>
> *First Amendment to the U.S. Constitution*

The basic foundation of our democracy is the First Amendment guarantee of freedom of expression. The Opposing Viewpoints series is dedicated to the concept of this basic freedom and the idea that it is more important to practice it than to enshrine it.

OPPOSING VIEWPOINTS® SERIES

America's Great Divide

Erica Grove, Book Editor

GREENHAVEN PUBLISHING

Published in 2023 by Greenhaven Publishing, LLC
2544 Clinton Street,
Buffalo NY 14224

Copyright © 2023 by Greenhaven Publishing, LLC

First Edition

All rights reserved. No part of this book may be reproduced in any form without permission in writing from the publisher, except by a reviewer.

Articles in Greenhaven Publishing anthologies are often edited for length to meet page requirements. In addition, original titles of these works are changed to clearly present the main thesis and to explicitly indicate the author's opinion. Every effort is made to ensure that Greenhaven Publishing accurately reflects the original intent of the authors. Every effort has been made to trace the owners of the copyrighted material.

Cover image: Trevor Bexon/Shutterstock.com

Library of Congress CataloginginPublication Data
Names: Grove, Erica M., editor.
Title: America's great divide / Erica Grove, book editor.
Description: First edition. | New York : Greenhaven Publishing, 2023. | Series: Opposing viewpoints | Includes bibliographical references and index. | Audience: Ages 15+ | Audience: Grades 10-12
Identifiers: LCCN 2022047765 | 9781534509221 (library binding) | ISBN 9781534509214 (paperback)
Subjects: LCSH: Polarization (Social sciences)--United States--Juvenile literature. | United States--Social conditions--21st century--Juvenile literature.
Classification: LCC HN90.P57 A64 2023 | DDC 306.0973--dc23/eng/20221117
LC record available at https://lccn.loc.gov/2022047765

Manufactured in the United States of America

Website: http://greenhavenpublishing.com

Contents

The Importance of Opposing Viewpoints	11
Introduction	14

Chapter 1: What Are the Main Sources of Division in Contemporary America?

Chapter Preface	18
1. The Urban-Rural Divide in America Keeps Growing *Alexandra Kanik and Patrick Scott*	20
2. America's Urban-Rural Divide Is Largely Exaggerated *Anne N. Junod, Clare Salerno, and Corianne Payton Scally*	27
3. Income Inequality Is the Main Driver of Division in American Society *Christos A. Makridis*	33
4. Race Is the Primary Cause of Political Division Today *Gregory Hood*	39
5. Cultural Differences and Partisan Identity Drive Division in America *Michael Dimock and Richard Wike*	45
6. Identity Politics Drive Social Change, Not Division *Alicia Garza*	50
Periodical and Internet Sources Bibliography	61

Chapter 2: Has America Become More Divided over Time?

Chapter Preface	64
1. Division in American Politics Is Not New *Lumen Learning*	66
2. Though the Government Is Divided, Americans Today Are Not Nearly as Divided as They Seem *Shawn Griffiths*	78
3. Political Violence Could Be on the Rise in America *Naomi Schalit and Ore Koren*	88

4.	Declining Trust in the Media Points to Greater Division *Jeffrey Gottfried and Jacob Liedke*	94
5.	Partisanship Has Become Part of Social Identity in America *Christopher McConnell, Yotam Margalit, Neil Malhotra, and Matthew Levendusky*	97
	Periodical and Internet Sources Bibliography	101

Chapter 3: Is America's Great Divide Unique?

	Chapter Preface	104
1.	America Is Polarizing Faster than Other Countries *Jill Kimball*	106
2.	Polarization Is Spreading Around the World *Thomas Carothers and Andrew O'Donohue*	110
3.	Certain Political Topics Are Far More Controversial in America than in Other Countries *David Lauter*	117
4.	America Is Not as Divided as It Seems *Ken Stern*	122
	Periodical and Internet Sources Bibliography	128

Chapter 4: Can America Become Less Divided?

	Chapter Preface	131
1.	Distrust in the Government and Other Americans Makes Reconciliation Challenging *Lee Rainie, Scott Keeter, and Andrew Perrin*	133
2.	Diagnosing and Addressing Polarized Psychology Can Help Fight Polarization *Beyond Conflict*	143
3.	Bridging the Political Divide Requires Tolerance and Cooperation, Not Friendship *Francesca Polletta*	148

4. Getting Rid of the Two-Party System Could
   Help America Overcome Its Divide **154**
   David A. Love
5. The Two-Party System Is an Essential Part of
   American Democracy **159**
   Alexander Cohen

Periodical and Internet Sources Bibliography **163**

For Further Discussion **165**
Organizations to Contact **167**
Bibliography of Books **171**
Index **173**

The Importance of Opposing Viewpoints

Perhaps every generation experiences a period in time in which the populace seems especially polarized, starkly divided on the important issues of the day and gravitating toward the far ends of the political spectrum and away from a consensus-facilitating middle ground. The world that today's students are growing up in and that they will soon enter into as active and engaged citizens is deeply fragmented in just this way. Issues relating to terrorism, immigration, women's rights, minority rights, race relations, health care, taxation, wealth and poverty, the environment, policing, military intervention, the proper role of government—in some ways, perennial issues that are freshly and uniquely urgent and vital with each new generation—are roiling the world.

If we are to foster a knowledgeable, responsible, active, and engaged citizenry among today's youth, we must provide them with the intellectual, interpretive, and critical-thinking tools and experience necessary to make sense of the world around them and of the all-important debates and arguments that inform it. After all, the outcome of these debates will in large measure determine the future course, prospects, and outcomes of the world and its people, particularly its youth. If they are to become successful members of society and productive and informed citizens, students need to learn how to evaluate the strengths and weaknesses of someone else's arguments, how to sift fact from opinion and fallacy, and how to test the relative merits and validity of their own opinions against the known facts and the best possible available information. The landmark series Opposing Viewpoints has been providing students with just such critical-thinking skills and exposure to the debates surrounding society's most urgent contemporary issues for many years, and it continues to serve this essential role with undiminished commitment, care, and rigor.

The key to the series's success in achieving its goal of sharpening students' critical-thinking and analytic skills resides in its title—

Opposing Viewpoints. In every intriguing, compelling, and engaging volume of this series, readers are presented with the widest possible spectrum of distinct viewpoints, expert opinions, and informed argumentation and commentary, supplied by some of today's leading academics, thinkers, analysts, politicians, policy makers, economists, activists, change agents, and advocates. Every opinion and argument anthologized here is presented objectively and accorded respect. There is no editorializing in any introductory text or in the arrangement and order of the pieces. No piece is included as a "straw man," an easy ideological target for cheap point-scoring. As wide and inclusive a range of viewpoints as possible is offered, with no privileging of one particular political ideology or cultural perspective over another. It is left to each individual reader to evaluate the relative merits of each argument—as they see it, and with the use of ever-growing critical-thinking skills—and grapple with their own assumptions, beliefs, and perspectives to determine how convincing or successful any given argument is and how the reader's own stance on the issue may be modified or altered in response to it.

This process is facilitated and supported by volume, chapter, and selection introductions that provide readers with the essential context they need to begin engaging with the spotlighted issues, with the debates surrounding them, and with their own perhaps shifting or nascent opinions on them. In addition, guided reading and discussion questions encourage readers to determine the authors' point of view and purpose, interrogate and analyze the various arguments and their rhetoric and structure, evaluate the arguments' strengths and weaknesses, test their claims against available facts and evidence, judge the validity of the reasoning, and bring into clearer, sharper focus the reader's own beliefs and conclusions and how they may differ from or align with those in the collection or those of their classmates.

Research has shown that reading comprehension skills improve dramatically when students are provided with compelling, intriguing, and relevant "discussable" texts. The subject matter of

The Importance of Opposing Viewpoints

these collections could not be more compelling, intriguing, or urgently relevant to today's students and the world they are poised to inherit. The anthologized articles and the reading and discussion questions that are included with them also provide the basis for stimulating, lively, and passionate classroom debates. Students who are compelled to anticipate objections to their own argument and identify the flaws in those of an opponent read more carefully, think more critically, and steep themselves in relevant context, facts, and information more thoroughly. In short, using discussable text of the kind provided by every single volume in the Opposing Viewpoints series encourages close reading, facilitates reading comprehension, fosters research, strengthens critical thinking, and greatly enlivens and energizes classroom discussion and participation. The entire learning process is deepened, extended, and strengthened.

For all of these reasons, Opposing Viewpoints continues to be exactly the right resource at exactly the right time—when we most need to provide readers with the critical-thinking tools and skills that will not only serve them well in school but also in their careers and their daily lives as decision-making family members, community members, and citizens. This series encourages respectful engagement with and analysis of opposing viewpoints and fosters a resulting increase in the strength and rigor of one's own opinions and stances. As such, it helps make readers "future ready," and that readiness will pay rich dividends for the readers themselves, for the citizenry, for our society, and for the world at large.

Introduction

> "Partisanship is our great curse. We too readily assume that everything has two sides and that it is our duty to be on one or the other."
>
> —James Harvey Robinson,
> American historian

According to a poll conducted in August 2022 by the *Economist* and the analytics firm YouGov, 43 percent of Americans believe that a civil war will occur within the next decade.[1] In this same poll, two-thirds of Americans stated that they believed political division had gotten worse in recent years.[2] Recent acts of political violence like the attack on the U.S. Capitol building on January 6, 2021, suggest that political tension is at a boiling point. However, explaining why the country is so divided is a complicated issue. This is because a number of issues divide Americans, including economic class, race, religion, political affiliation, education, culture, and geography. For this reason, experts, politicians, and members of the public alike have all attempted to determine which factors play the largest role in America's great divide and find solutions to bridge this divide.

In many ways, division and partisanship are not new issues in the United States. Since its origins, the United States has been a two-party system, with the Federalists and Anti-Federalists serving as the initial two parties before the Republicans and Democrats dominated.[3] Because of the size of the country and the large number of voters in a national election, the relative simplicity of a two-party election—in which voters simply have to choose between candidates from the two dominant parties—made it an

Introduction

attractive option.[4] However, critics of the two-party system argue that it causes hyper-polarization, in which people who align with one political party are pitted against those who align with the other. It creates an antagonistic relationship between voters from each political party. A 2022 poll by the Pew Research Center found that 65 percent of Republicans and 54 percent of Democrats held very unfavorable views of the other party.[5] This is significantly higher than the findings from 1994, when only 21 percent of Republicans and 17 percent of Democrats reported that level of antipathy.[6]

There are many issues that play a role in dividing Americans, from race, to economic class, to religious beliefs, to geography. The viewpoints in this volume examine the cause-and-effect relationship between political polarization and these related issues in an effort to better understand how division as a whole in America can be addressed. As Thomas Carothers and Andrew O'Donohue put it, polarization in America is so unique and so strong because it "is the powerful alignment of ethnicity, ideology, and religion on each side of the divide—what we call the 'iron triangle' of U.S. polarization."[8] While it is unclear whether these issues are responsible for political division, it is clear that they have a strong relationship to it of some nature.

But just as there are many possible causes for America's great divide, there are also many potential solutions that experts and politicians have identified to help address it. One of these is restructuring America's political system to allow for more than two parties, which some believe could help reduce political polarization. Others suggest promoting civility among Americans of all political and cultural backgrounds by encouraging conversation and understanding. Still others think that renewing faith in America's political system is the key, and believe that politicians should prioritize increasing trust among voters from both parties.

In chapters titled "What Are the Main Sources of Division in Contemporary America?" "Has America Become More Divided over Time?" "Is America's Great Divide Unique?" and "Can Americans Become Less Divided?" the expert viewpoints presented in *Opposing Viewpoints: America's Great Divide* explore the issue of the rift in American politics and society from a wide range of angles. They examine to what extent this division is rooted in American history, what factors in society and politics played a role in creating it, and how to help American society become less divided.

Notes

1. Taylor Orth, "Two in five Americans say a civil war is at least somewhat likely in the next decade," YouGov America, August 26, 2022. https://today.yougov.com/topics/politics/articles-reports/2022/08/26/two-in-five-americans-civil-war-somewhat-likely.
2. *Ibid.*
3. Editors of Encyclopaedia Britannica, "Two-Party Systems," *Encyclopaedia Britannica*, n.d. https://www.britannica.com/topic/political-party/Two-party-systems.
4. *Ibid.*
5. "As Partisan Hostility Grows, Signs of Frustration With the Two-Party System," August 9, 2022. https://www.pewresearch.org/politics/2022/08/09/as-partisan-hostility-grows-signs-of-frustration-with-the-two-party-system/.
6. *Ibid.*
7. Thomas Carothers and Andrew O'Donohue, "How to Understand the Global Spread of Political Polarization," Carnegie Endowment for International Peace, October 1, 2019. https://carnegieendowment.org/2019/10/01/how-to-understand-global-spread-of-political-polarization-pub-79893.

OPPOSING VIEWPOINTS® SERIES

CHAPTER 1

What Are the Main Sources of Division in Contemporary America?

VIEWPOINT 1

> "This election has shown that urban and rural voters in the U.S. have grown yet further apart when it comes to their political preferences."

The Urban-Rural Divide in America Keeps Growing

Alexandra Kanik and Patrick Scott

This viewpoint by Alexandra Kanik and Patrick Scott analyzes the results of the 2020 U.S. presidential election. It examines data on how voters in urban and rural areas voted and compares it to data from the 2016 presidential election. It found that voters in urban areas of all sizes voted Democrat at higher rates than in the previous election. This indicates that the urban-rural divide—in which urban voters vote Democrat at high rates, while rural voters vote Republican—has grown. This leads to greater polarization between people who live in urban and rural areas. Alexandra Kanik was a data reporter for City Monitor. *Patrick Scott is the projects editor on the New Statesman Media Group's data journalism team.*

As you read, consider the following questions:

1. Where did bigger swings in Democratic votes occur in the 2020 presidential election, according to this viewpoint?
2. What does MSA stand for?

"The Urban-Rural Divide Only Deepened in the 2020 US Election," by Alexandra Kanik and Patrick Scott, City Monitor, November 11, 2020. Reprinted by permission.

3. How did Trump's margins change in large metro areas between the 2016 and 2020 elections?

The results of the 2020 U.S. presidential election show a widening urban-rural divide in U.S. politics, according to an analysis of preliminary election results by *City Monitor*.

Heavily urban areas have long been associated with larger shares of Democratic voting, but the results of this year's election show that this relationship is becoming more extreme, with bigger swings in the vote towards the Democrats tending to occur in more densely populated counties.

By looking at "swing," we're analysing the change in the performance of the Democrats, as defined by their vote share, relative to the same metric for the Republicans. This is a method more generally used in multiparty systems such as in the UK but makes sense in the 2020 U.S. presidential election because both major parties saw increases in vote share this year. The vote can swing to a party without that party winning in that area—it is an indicator of progress or regression.

Based on this measure, President-elect Joe Biden saw more favourable margins between his share of the vote and President Donald Trump's in 47 percent of counties across the U.S. when compared to the latter's margins against Hillary Clinton in 2016, according to results data reported by the *New York Times*.

Break down that data by urban/rural status and a more divided picture emerges.

Throughout this article, we will refer to counties in metropolitan statistical areas, or MSAs, of 1 million population or more as large metro areas. Counties in MSAs of with between 250,000 and 999,999 people will be called medium metro areas. Counties in MSAs of fewer than 250,000 population will be called small metro areas, and all other counties will be referred to as rural areas.

Trump's margins worsened in 74 percent of large metro areas, per our definition above. Included in this group are counties that encompass major city areas such as New York County, New

York (otherwise known as Manhattan), and Los Angeles County, California, as well as inner- and outer-ring suburban counties such as Collin County, Texas, near Dallas, and Stafford County, Virginia, an exurb outside of Washington, DC. As you travel farther away from densely populated cities, Trump's margins fared better. In the most rural parts of the U.S., only 36 percent of counties saw Trump's margins get worse compared with 2016 numbers.

These shifts mean the Democrats' overall lead in large metro areas increased to a margin of 14 percentage points among counties where at least 90 percent of the expected vote have been counted. This is up from an 11.6-point lead in 2016 and a 0.8-point lead in 2004.

Rural America Is Underserved by Politicians and Philanthropists

Ask Americans what parts of the country are the most poverty-stricken, and they will probably talk about cities like Cleveland, Baltimore, and St. Louis. They aren't likely to mention rural areas in states like Mississippi, New Mexico, and Arkansas.

Yet the rate of poverty is significantly higher in rural America than it is in urban America. According to the most recent data from the federal government, in 2018 the poverty rate in metropolitan areas was 12.6 percent, while the poverty rate in nonmetropolitan areas was 16.1 percent, more than 25 percent higher.

And poverty is just one of the areas where there is a divide between urban and rural. Rural areas have fewer cultural institutions, fewer colleges and universities, fewer nonprofit organizations, fewer social services, fewer jobs—the list goes on.

Given this disparity, you would think that philanthropists would be pouring money into rural areas. Sadly, that's not the case. In fact, it's the opposite. Philanthropists have been putting much more money into urban areas.

What Are the Main Sources of Division in Contemporary America?

Meanwhile, the vote in midsize and small metro areas also swung to the Democrats after two elections in which they lost ground in these counties. These areas are generally still majority-Republican, but 61 percent of them saw swings to Biden this election.

It is important to note that while Trump's margins shifted in many counties, not all of them "turned blue" this year. Of the 1,246 counties that swung to Biden, Trump held on to 79 percent of them.

It's possible, however, that this picture could change when the final tallies are in.

According to a U.S. government study of more than 1,200 of the largest U.S. foundations, "the average real value of grants from large foundations to organizations based in nonmetro counties from 2005 to 2010 was about $88 per capita (in 2010 dollars), less than half the average ($192 per capita) given to organizations in metro counties."

Why do so many U.S. philanthropists ignore rural areas, and what can be done to remedy the gap? Those are the questions that the authors of "Philanthropy's Rural Blind Spot" seek to answer in the cover story in this Spring 2021 issue of *Stanford Social Innovation Review*.

One of the reasons for the giving gap is that the largest U.S. foundations are mostly based in urban areas. Of the 10 U.S. foundations with the largest endowments, all but the W. K. Kellogg Foundation (Battle Creek, Michigan) and Robert Wood Johnson Foundation (Princeton, New Jersey) are based in large metropolitan areas.

There are, of course, community foundations based in rural areas, but they are smaller than their urban peers. For the most part, private foundations and corporate philanthropy exist in an urban bubble, largely isolated from the rest of the country.

"The Urban and Rural Divide," by Eric Nee, Stanford Social Innovation Review, Spring 2021.

Better Performance Near Cities Helped Biden Flip Key States

Even though Biden didn't flip hundreds of individual counties, based on the data we have so far, movements towards Biden in areas surrounding large cities were crucial in flipping states such as Pennsylvania.

Biden's home state saw 10 of its 13 large metro-area counties, mostly made up of suburban and exurban areas, and 13 of its 14 medium metro counties swing towards Biden, even though Trump still held the edge in some of them. Of course, winning counties doesn't translate into Electoral College votes, but these multiple small shifts towards Biden are likely to have been a key reason why Pennsylvania turned blue overall.

Many of these medium metro areas are in the eastern part of the state, between Philadelphia and Harrisburg, and include the counties of Lancaster and York, where Biden achieved a quarter more votes than Clinton.

What is interesting in these areas is that the improved performance of the Democrats in Pennsylvania was not obviously achieved by changing the minds of those who voted for Trump in 2016. He achieved more votes compared with four years ago in all 14 of the state's counties classified as medium metro areas, but all 14 still swung towards Biden.

A similar pattern can be observed in Virginia, another state that Biden flipped. Stafford County, an outer-ring suburban county about 40 miles south of Washington, DC, saw Trump margins shift by 12 points this election when compared with the last one, dropping him low enough to lose, with only 47.5 percent of the vote to Biden's 50.8 percent.

Urban Areas Moved Towards the Democrats in Red States Too

This shift towards Biden in medium and small metro areas—driven largely, it seems, by the Democrats' benefiting more from turnout increases—can also be seen in states that did not turn blue on election night.

For example, Trump won in Collin County, Texas, which contains the northeast corner of Dallas and the city of McKinney. In 2016, Trump won in Collin with 55.6 percent of the vote. This election, he was able to bring in only 51 percent.

Again, this change looks to have been driven by greater voter turnout rather than wholesale switching between the two major parties. Those numbers are still preliminary, but compared with the 2016 election, Collin saw nearly 126,000 additional votes, an increase of 35 percent. The population of the county has also increased by nearly 10 percent since 2016.

While changes in many small and medium metro areas didn't result in Biden "flipping" counties, Trump did lose some of those he won in 2016. Tarrant County, Texas, the urban county that is home to Fort Worth, saw Biden sneak by with 49.3 percent of the vote, compared with Trump's 49.1 percent. While experiencing a mere 4 percent increase in population between 2016 and 2019, Tarrant saw a 24 percent increase in votes cast this election. As of this writing, the *New York Times* estimates that 96 percent of votes have been counted there.

Williamson County, Texas, a suburban county outside of Austin, saw Trump's margins shift by 11 percentage points, dropping his 48.2% share of the vote just below Biden's 49.5%.

Is This Good News for Cities?

It's tempting to view the fact that a Democrat has won the 2020 presidential election as good news for the political representation of people living in cities; however, there are reasons to be cautious.

City Monitor examined this issue in an interview with Stanford University professor Jonathan Rodden, author of *Why Cities Lose*, before the election. He highlighted the danger of Democratic politicians' ignoring the growing polarisation of politics along urban-rural lines in the event that they win the presidency.

The danger for cities is that national politicians do little to address the fact that, electorally, urban voters are at a big disadvantage in the US's winner-take-all system. The Republican

Party won the Electoral College without winning the popular vote in 2016, and it could be argued that a potentially unsustainable level of turnout was one of the main factors that prevented this happening again in 2020.

"A lot of this gets papered over when you have a big blue wave," explained Rodden. "As the Republican Party has lost support in many suburbs, the entire problem we've been talking about may be diminishing. In that case, Democrats might come to the conclusion it's not a problem at all anymore. Over time, they might be correct in that assessment. As the political geography changes – and it's really changing quite dramatically – the problem may be going away. Or it might just be going into hibernation for a little while and then it shows up again a few years later."

This election has shown that urban and rural voters in the US have grown yet further apart when it comes to their political preferences. Neglecting to address this divide through electoral reform now might mean the problem comes back with a vengeance in future elections.

VIEWPOINT 2

> *"To improve the accuracy and relevance of rural reporting, journalists and researchers can eschew rural myths, represent the diversities of rural places, and focus on rural-specific experiences with issues common to all communities."*

America's Urban-Rural Divide Is Largely Exaggerated

Anne N. Junod, Clare Salerno, and Corianne Payton Scally

According to the authors of this viewpoint, the urban-rural divide is not nearly as pronounced as the media and scholarly reporting would suggest. This inaccurate reporting presents rural areas as homogenous, white areas with a culture of poverty. They suggest that voters in these areas all have the same political beliefs and vote the same way. These depictions are inaccurate and drive a greater sense of division between people in urban and rural areas. Instead of viewing political issues as either "urban" issues or "rural" issues, the authors suggest realizing and acknowledging that people in these areas face many of the same issues and deserve the same amount of support. Anne Junod is a research associate in the Metropolitan Housing and Communities Policy Center at the Urban Institute, where Corianne Payton Scally is a senior fellow. Clare Selarno is a former research analyst for the Urban Institute.

"Debunking Three Myths about Rural America," by Anne N. Junod, Clare Salerno, and Corianne Payton Scally, The Urban Institute, October 30, 2020. Reprinted by permission.

As you read, consider the following questions:

1. According to this viewpoint, what percent of rural Americans are people of color?
2. What is the main driver of economic challenges in rural areas, according to this viewpoint?
3. What are the three recommendations the authors give to help strengthen research and reporting on rural areas?

News media and scholarly reporting frequently misrepresent or misunderstand rural America. Few examples illustrate this more than the wake of the 2016 election, when droves of largely nonrural reporters flocked to rural communities to find out what happened.

Although much has been written critiquing such drive-by journalism, narrow and reductive depictions of rural America persist. This storytelling contributes to growing mistrust of outside researchers and reporters, and the oft-described rural-urban divide erases rural diversities and unduly polarizes differences between cities and small towns.

With more local newsrooms closing, local perspectives on rural stories are told less often, and the most negative stories from nonlocal reporters rise to the top. Although two-thirds of 2016 Donald Trump voters were neither poor nor working class, and although small city and suburban voters played a greater role in Trump's victory than rural voters, most national media still focus on rural voters and circulate tropes of rural Americans as largely white, uneducated, working-class farmers.

To improve the accuracy and relevance of rural reporting, journalists and researchers can eschew rural myths, represent the diversities of rural places, and focus on rural-specific experiences with issues common to all communities. Here we debunk three myths about rural America and provide recommendations for reporters and researchers engaging rural communities during the 2020 election cycle and beyond.

Myth: Rural America is the white, agricultural "heartland."

Fact: Rural America is increasingly diverse.

One in five Americans lives in rural communities, and more than one in five (22 percent) rural residents are people of color. Rural Native American, Asian, and Latinx groups are growing fastest, followed by African Americans with modest population gains, and non-Hispanic white groups experiencing the slowest growth. Most rural Americans are not farmers—in fact, fewer than 6 percent of rural Americans are employed in agriculture. The largest employers are the education, health care, and social assistance sectors, followed by retail, construction, and transportation. And rural communities exist in nearly every state and territory, not just the Midwest.

Stereotypes about rural America as the white, agricultural heartland perpetuate the myth of the rural idyll, in which rural places are depicted as aspirational, largely white farming communities set apart from modern life. This myth erases the historical and growing diversity of rural places, masks real and persistent rural challenges, and miscasts rural ways of life as antiquated or regressed.

Myth: Poor, rural people live in "cultures of poverty."

Fact: Most chronic economic challenges in rural areas occur because of changing global economies.

Consequences of globalization—including manufacturing losses, economic restructuring, extractive industry monopolization, and agricultural consolidation—have contributed to economic decline and social disruption in many, though certainly not all, rural places. Instead of reflecting such realities, reporting about these communities often scapegoats residents as having intergenerational social or moral deficiencies that entrench them in "cultures of poverty."

America's Great Divide

continue to disappear and rural myths persist, researchers and reporters can strengthen the quality and accuracy of rural reporting by avoiding stereotypes, meaningfully engaging rural stakeholders, and elevating the diversity, assets, and challenges of rural places.

VIEWPOINT 3

> "The evidence indicates not only a strong correlation between income inequality and political polarization but also potential causality: Greater income inequality can amplify political tensions by raising polarization."

Income Inequality Is the Main Driver of Division in American Society

Christos A. Makridis

In the following viewpoint, which was published around the time of the 2016 U.S. presidential election, Christos A. Makridis examines the relationship between political polarization and income inequality. It explains that political polarization is at its highest point in recent history, and that the gap between the richest and poorest Americans has also grown. While it is difficult to determine which factor is causing the other, the author argues that it is most likely income inequality that is driving political polarization. Gaps in income take a long time to develop, which makes it less likely to be swayed by polarization. Greater income inequality causes political tensions to grow, which results in polarization. Addressing income inequality is an important step in bridging the divide. Christos A. Makridis is a research professor at Arizona State University.

"Are Soaring Levels of Income Inequality Making Us a More Polarized Nation?" by Christos A. Makridis, The Conversation, August 5, 2016. https://theconversation.com/are-soaring-levels-of-income-inequality-making-us-a-more-polarized-nation-63418. Licensed under CC BY-4.0 International.

America's Great Divide

As you read, consider the following questions:

1. What is the source of the data Christos A. Makridis uses in this viewpoint?
2. How does a 1 percent rise in the earnings gap relate to political polarization?
3. What are the negative consequences of political polarization the author mentions?

Political polarization today is greater than it's been in recent history—at least since the 1970s. To see that, one need only look at the current U.S. presidential election.

And whatever your political leanings, an overly divided country can hamper its progress, such as the ability to innovate or adapt to geopolitical risk.

Another trend that has emerged over the same period is the widening gap between the richest and poorest Americans. By some estimates, it's the widest it's ever been.

These two coinciding facts raise the tantalizing question: Did the rise of income inequality over the past three decades contribute to increased political polarization? Or is it the other way around? Or perhaps it's just a coincidence that they both have climbed over the same 30-40 year period?

Chicken and the Egg?

Unfortunately, causality—and its direction—can be very difficult to show, although intuitively we can see how either one might affect the other.

For example, greater income inequality may generate more polarization because disparities in earnings affect our priorities. It's been argued that as we make more or less money, the issues we care about most change, as do how we feel about those issues.

On the other hand, greater polarization can generate gridlock in government, making it more difficult to pass legislation. If, for example, there are pressing issues, then greater dispersion in

What Are the Main Sources of Division in Contemporary America?

attitudes might make agreement more difficult. Inaction could, in theory, curtail efforts aimed at addressing inequality.

While both are plausible, my view is that the former mechanism is more likely—greater income inequality is leading to more polarization—because earnings inequality is not a transitory relationship. Rather, big differences in earnings takes years to develop, and the bulk of income inequality is explained by longer-run factors. For causality to work the other way, contemporary polarized voting patterns would have to be affecting inequality, which seems unlikely.

Furthermore, recent research in political science has also pushed back on conventional theories that polarization hinders the passage of policy.

Understanding the direction of causality is important for policy. If income inequality is the cause, we should not expect political compromises until labor force participation and competitiveness rise—reducing inequality. If polarization is the cause, then we should not expect our economy to improve until we are able to compromise.

Diving into the Data

These questions prompted me to gather data from the Current Population Survey (CPS) and Gallup from 2008 to 2015.

The CPS is a survey frequently used by economists to understand changing demographics and employment outcomes throughout the U.S. economy with fresh snapshots every month. The Bureau of Labor Statistics uses the data to compile its monthly unemployment report.

Gallup, arguably the largest polling organization in the U.S., regularly surveys individuals on a range of issues, including their political ideology.

Before we go any further, we need to agree on some definitions. First, although political polarization does not have a uniform definition, I define it here as the fraction of people reporting that they are extreme liberal minus those reporting as extreme

2. What is the best predictor of one's attitude toward the Democratic Party, according to this viewpoint?
3. How many studies did the authors of the paper referenced in this viewpoint conduct to support their claims?

Political commentators are noticing that the two major American political parties are diverging and becoming more hostile to each other. Why?

According to an award-winning paper from political scientists Nicholas Valentino and Kirill Zhirkov, race is more important than ideology in determining party affiliation. They argue that race and partisan identification are linked in the minds of Americans, with "Republican" and "Democrat" beginning to stand for "white" and "non-white." Even as many Republicans claim to oppose it, future politics will be identity politics.

The dry academic prose of this report belies its explosive conclusions. The authors argue (full paper here) that "racial and partisan schemas" increasingly overlap and drive increasing polarization—and they do so more than other group identities such as class, religion, or ideology.

The current leading explanation for polarization, advanced by scholars such as Professor Lilliana Mason in Uncivil Agreement, is that internal disagreements within the parties are disappearing, resulting in Republicans and Democrats disagreeing with each other on more issues. In other words, there are fewer pro-lifers, gun-owning Democrats, and fewer big government, welfare supporting Republicans. The authors of this new paper find a more fundamental reason for the political divide. Prof. Valentino and Mr. Zhirkov argue that racial differences between the parties or, more specifically, the "racial images that we have in our head" drive polarization.

"We demonstrate that the two parties have diverged dramatically in terms of their racial composition and, most importantly, due to the rapid decline in the numbers of whites in the Democratic

Party," said Mr. Zhirkov in a recently posted video. "Over time, this gap in racial composition makes the best predictor of the affective distance between Democrats and Republicans. It works even better than ideological sorting, for instance."

The authors argue that increasing polarization and the negative opinion Republicans and Democrats hold of each other "springs from a mental image of the opposition that is composed of disliked social groups," including different races. As both parties become more racially homogeneous, fewer American voters ever hear a dissenting opinion from within their party, and therefore develop more extreme in-group and out-group attitudes.

The authors argue that partisan identity can develop independently from social group identity but only among a narrow group of "well-informed, highly interested voters." The rest "derive their partisan attachments from their social group membership." In other words, there are a few, very politically involved people whose politics reflect ideas; for the rest, politics reflect their social group, the most salient of which is race.

The authors don't say so, but, the "well-informed, highly interested voters" with partisan identities separate from social group probably include many of the professional "conservative movement" activists who have labored so hard to keep white identity politics verboten within the GOP—as well as the dwindling number of white men who are still Democrats despite the party's sharp tilt against them.

Unfortunately for conservatives like these who thought Barack Obama's election would remove the "race card" from the Left's arsenal, the authors cite significant evidence that "the country's first African-American president polarized the electorate and increased opposition to left-wing policies among racially conservative whites (Tesler 2016), may have increased racial resentment (Valentino and Brader 2011), and even boosted the acceptability of explicitly hostile racial rhetoric in the most recent campaigns (Valentino, Neuner, and Vandenbroek 2016)." Thus, the authors believe recent history has changed the most common view of both parties "such that Democrats are not simply viewed as liberal but are quite automatically viewed as non-white" while "Republicans, on the other hand, are viewed primarily as a party of whites."

The authors conducted three studies that support their claims. The first study found attitudes about race are increasingly the best predictor of how close someone feels to the Democrat Party. Scores on what is called the "racial resentment index" were better indicators of this than either values (pro-life versus pro-choice) or policy (support or oppose increased defense spending): "[R]ace and racial attitudes were strongly and increasingly associated with the growing affective polarization identified by others." The authors also found that racial attitudes were more important than "social identities based on religion or class."

Needless to say, there are problems with the "racial resentment index," which is calculated from the answers to four questions:

- "Irish, Italians, Jews, and many other minorities overcame prejudice and worked their way up. Blacks should do the same without any special favors."
- "Generations of slavery and discrimination have created conditions that make it difficult for blacks to work their way out of the lower class."
- "Over the past few years, blacks have gotten less than they deserve."
- "It's really a matter of some people not trying hard enough; if blacks would only try harder they could be just as well off as whites."

Obviously, what is being measured is the level of sympathy for blacks, not "resentment," and the fourth question is actually two different questions that some people cannot answer with a single "yes" or "no." Race realists may think that blacks do not try hard enough and therefore answer "yes" to the first part of the fourth question (and therefore would be considered unsympathetic to blacks), but they also know that because of race differences blacks as a group can't be "just as well off as whites" and therefore answer "no." A "no" answer would be scored as "sympathetic" because the implication is that blacks are held back by society, not their own limitations. There are other problems with the index that go far beyond this paper, but it is still significant that answers to these four questions are an increasingly good indicator of how strongly someone identifies as a Democrat or Republican.

The authors' second study used a test designed to measure implicit racial bias to see how strongly someone associates Republicans and Democrats with blacks or whites. Conclusion: "A substantial proportion of Republicans very strongly associated the Republican Party with whites and the Democratic Party with blacks, while very few Democrats strongly associated the Republican Party with blacks." Scores on the "racial resentment index" were also good indicators of how Democrats and Republicans viewed the other party.

One could dispute this finding because it uses the implicit association test (IAT) developed by Project Implicit. This test and others like it have been used to claim that whites hold strong "implicit biases," and to justify the expensive "training" required to cure it. Yet even the creators of this test have admitted it does not predict biased behavior in the lab, let alone in the real world. A 2009 study published in the Journal of Personality of Social Psychology found the IAT does predict behavior and is more accurate than self-reporting, but a 2016 study found only a weak correlation between "implicit bias" and discriminatory behavior, and little evidence that changes in implicit bias change a person's behavior.

The authors' third study is the most interesting. After answering questions about their own background, respondents were asked to identify "the typical supporter" of both the Democrat and the Republican Party on the same identity dimensions they used to describe themselves. The subjects thought of Democrats as more racially diverse and slightly more working class, and Republicans as white, evangelical, and middle class or wealthy. However, the authors write that "only a racial match had an impact on partisan affective polarization [emotional attachment or hostility], whereas matching with a party in terms of religion and social class did not. . . ." In other words, being of the same race as the typical party member was more likely than similar religion or social class to predict emotional attachment to or hostility towards a party. Even after the authors controlled for respondents' positions on partisan issues, race was the best predictor of attachment or hostility. In summary: "Individuals do think of the two major U.S. parties in racial terms and those beliefs impact their feelings about partisans on either side of aisle. Explicit racial schemas also appear to be more powerful predictors of affective polarization than ones based on religion or class."

The authors conclude that over the entire course of American history, it has been race—not class, religion, or ideology—that "imbue[s] partisan disagreement with the kind of antipathy we are now witnessing." Echoing race realists, the authors say, "Racial animosity, perhaps more than any other identity cleavage, has defined and structured American politics." Peter Brimelow recently argued that the defeat of white Democrats in recent primaries shows the party has "tipped" towards non-whites, and Steve Sailer says the Democrats are in danger of being viewed as "the black party."

Race intensifies political polarization but does not determine it. White Democrats do not identify with white Republicans. As the authors note, some research suggests parents are more likely to be upset by a child marrying outside their political party than outside their race. Also, whites are still a plurality of Democratic voters. However, the two parties' views of racial issues and the racialized images partisans have of their rivals are fueling radicalization. "Race" and "party" will increasingly merge if trends continue.

White advocates are right to think race is the most important factor in American politics. If polarization continues, white advocacy will become mainstream, at least among Republicans. President Trump was just the beginning.

VIEWPOINT 5

> "Race, religion and ideology now align with partisan identity in ways that they often didn't in eras when the two parties were relatively heterogenous coalitions."

Cultural Differences and Partisan Identity Drive Division in America

Michael Dimock and Richard Wike

Although political polarization is not an issue that is unique to the United States, Michael Dimock and Richard Wike argue that there are characteristics of America's polarization that make it different from—and worse than—polarization in other countries. The two-party system plays a role in this division by collapsing social and political debates into a fight between two different groups. Furthermore, what makes this divide so pronounced is how many aspects of one's social and cultural identity are stacked onto their political identity, including their race, religion, and ideologies. This makes political identity uniquely multifaceted and encompassing compared to other countries. Michael Dimock is president of the Pew Research Center, where Richard Wike is director of global attitudes research.

"America Is Exceptional in the Nature of Its Political Divide," by Michael Dimock and Richard Wike, Pew Research Center, November 13, 2020. Reprinted with permission.

America's Great Divide

As you read, consider the following questions:

1. What is the percentage gap between Republicans who approved of how the government was addressing the COVID-19 in early 2020 and Democrats who approved?
2. What makes polarization in America so encompassing, according to this viewpoint?
3. Why do the authors argue that we should not be entirely nostalgic for less polarized times?

In his first speech as president-elect, Joe Biden made clear his intention to bridge the deep and bitter divisions in American society. He pledged to look beyond red and blue and to discard the harsh rhetoric that characterizes our political debates.

It will be a difficult struggle. Americans have rarely been as polarized as they are today.

The studies we've conducted at Pew Research Center over the past few years illustrate the increasingly stark disagreement between Democrats and Republicans on the economy, racial justice, climate change, law enforcement, international engagement and a long list of other issues. The 2020 presidential election further highlighted these deep-seated divides. Supporters of Biden and Donald Trump believe the differences between them are about more than just politics and policies. A month before the election, roughly eight-in-ten registered voters in both camps said their differences with the other side were about core American values, and roughly nine-in-ten—again in both camps—worried that a victory by the other would lead to "lasting harm" to the United States.

The U.S. is hardly the only country wrestling with deepening political fissures. Brexit has polarized British politics, the rise of populist parties has disrupted party systems across Europe, and cultural conflict and economic anxieties have intensified old cleavages and created new ones in many advanced democracies. America and other advanced economies face many common strains over how opportunity is distributed in a global economy and how our culture adapts to growing diversity in an interconnected world.

But the 2020 pandemic has revealed how pervasive the divide in American politics is relative to other nations. Over the summer, 76% of Republicans (including independents who lean to the party) felt the U.S. had done a good job dealing with the coronavirus outbreak, compared with just 29% of those who do not identify with the Republican Party. This 47 percentage point gap was the largest gap found between those who support the governing party and those who do not across 14 nations surveyed. Moreover, 77% of Americans said the country was now more divided than before the outbreak, as compared with a median of 47% in the 13 other nations surveyed.

Much of this American exceptionalism preceded the coronavirus: In a Pew Research Center study conducted before the pandemic, Americans were more ideologically divided than any of the 19 other publics surveyed when asked how much trust they have in scientists and whether scientists make decisions solely based on facts. These fissures have pervaded nearly every aspect of the public and policy response to the crisis over the course of the year. Democrats and Republicans differ over mask wearing, contact tracing, how well public health officials are dealing with the crisis, whether to get a vaccine once one is available, and whether life will remain changed in a major way after the pandemic. For Biden supporters, the coronavirus outbreak was a central issue in the election—in an October poll, 82% said it was very important to their vote. Among Trump supporters, it was easily the least significant among six issues tested on the survey: Just 24% said it was very important.

Why is America cleaved in this way? Once again, looking across other nations gives us some indication. The polarizing pressures of partisan media, social media, and even deeply rooted cultural, historical and regional divides are hardly unique to America. By comparison, America's relatively rigid, two-party electoral system stands apart by collapsing a wide range of legitimate social and

VIEWPOINT 6

> "Identity politics is a threat to those who hold and wield power, because it destabilizes the control against which all else is compared."

Identity Politics Drive Social Change, Not Division

Alicia Garza

In the following viewpoint, Alicia Garza argues that despite the bad reputation identity politics have received in recent years as a source of division, when identity politics are rooted in shifting the balance of power, they can be an important force for social and political change. Identity politics examine the ways in which race, class, and gender are connected and how they affect one's experience of living in America. They also examine the unequal and unjust assumptions about what defines the "standard" American experience and how this impacts people who deviate from that. Garza argues that the fight against identity politics is intended to maintain the political and social status quo. Alicia Garza is a civil rights activist, writer, and cofounder of the international Black Lives Matter movement.

As you read, consider the following questions:

1. Who came up with the term "identity politics"?

"Identity Politics: Friend or Foe?" by Alicia Garza, University of California, Berkeley, September 24, 2019. Reprinted by permission.

2. According to this viewpoint, on average how does the wealth of white households compare to Black households?
3. What is one example Alicia Garza gives to demonstrate that whiteness is considered the standard, or "normal," in America?

The term "identity politics" was first coined by Black feminist Barbara Smith and the Combahee River Collective in 1974. Identity politics originated from the need to reshape movements that had until then prioritized the monotony of sameness over the strategic value of difference.

The "second wave" feminist movement fought for body autonomy, pushed for women's equality and demanded that women be treated as human beings. However, much like the first wave of feminism, which was largely centered around women's suffrage and gaining the right to vote, white women became the default standard for all women.

While segregation was no longer formally the law of the land in 1974, racism and discrimination based on class was still deeply embedded in efforts to achieve change, again, because the change desired was progress for white women and not all women. Women who identified as feminists were encouraged to join together on the basis of a common experience of discrimination based on sex, with no attention paid to the fact that not all women's experiences were the same, and further, that sex was not a category that could adequately describe gender.

This is the context for the emergence of identity politics. Stated simply, identity politics is the assertion that "the most profound and potentially most radical politics come directly out of our own identity, as opposed to working to end somebody else's oppression."[1] The Combahee River Collective detailed how their experiences as Black women were different than those of white women, and this mattered because understanding the ways in which racial, economic, gender, and other oppressions were linked and shaped their lives helped to make sure that no one could be left behind.

The purpose of this paper is to explore "identity politics" and whether or not it is a useful tool for civic engagement and movements today. In this paper, I argue that identity politics is not only widely misunderstood, but intentionally distorted in order to avoid acknowledging the ways in which "identity" shapes the economy, our democracy, and our society. I explore the Black feminist origins of identity politics, and explore how and why identity politics is being weaponized among progressives and conservatives—and with what consequences for increased participation by marginalized groups in mainstream politics.

Ultimately, I argue that identity politics is indeed a critical tool for organizing and civic engagement. Recognizing oneself and one's experiences in politics is a motivating factor for participation in that which is political. At a moment when America is facing some of the sharpest political polarization that it has seen in decades, anyone looking to secure the participation of marginalized groups had better start acknowledging that they're marginalized in the first place, and second, working to design policy solutions that leave no one behind.

What We Get Wrong about Identity Politics

Leaving no one behind is ideal, and, despite the best intentions, people are always getting left behind in social movements—particularly when the differences that emerge as a result of various forms of oppression are erased or intentionally ignored.

Social change work is a series of scientific experiments. In experiments, to determine whether or not change has occurred, you have to have a control. The control in a scientific experiment is, by definition, a sample that remains the same through an experiment. The control helps you to determine whether or not change has happened. The control must remain the same or equal at all times to ensure accurate measurement of results.

What Are the Main Sources of Division in Contemporary America?

In social change movements in America, the control is often based on the progress that white people are making in their lives against a white standard. In the women's movement, for example, the measure of progress is taken as whether or not change and progress is happening in the lives of white women.

It's well known that there is a lack of parity in wages between cisgender (people for whom their gender assigned at birth matches their gender identity) men and women. On average, cisgender women make 85 cents to every dollar a cisgender man makes.2 Women of all racial and ethnic groups make less than their male counterparts, and also make less than white men. Black women make 65.3 cents to every dollar that a white man makes, and 89 cents to every dollar a Black man makes. Latinx women make 61.6 cents to every dollar that a white man makes, and 85.7 percent of what a Latinx man makes. Among Latinx transgender and gender non-conforming people, 28 percent reported making less than $10,000 a year, and 34 percent of Black transgender and gender non-conforming people report the same.3

It is significant that discussions of the gender wage gap often start off with the assumption that all women make 85 cents to every dollar men make, since that is only true for white women. Without this qualification, one might think that all women make 80 cents to each dollar a man makes. Time and time again, the experiences of white communities are used as the framework from which to understand inequality, and yet the communities experiencing inequality from a range of factors, all at the same time, are communities of color. From abortion rights to pay equity, comparing the conditions of white women to white men has been the way to assess whether or not change is actually happening and progress is being made.

Identity politics holds us accountable to ask more questions about for whom progress is being made. The significant gaps in wages for Black and Latinx women indicate that while some are making progress, others continue to lag behind.

Identity politics says that no longer should we be expected to fight against someone else's oppression without fighting against our own, too. The Combahee River Collective was concerned with how our lived experiences shape our lives, and identity politics offered social movements, like the women's movement, the gift of uncovering what had been ignored or devalued. Black women who were poor and working class wanted feminism as much as white middle-class women did. Identity politics not only showed Black women that we were worthy of feminism—worthy of being treated as human beings—but it also gave white middle class women the gift of understanding that for feminism to succeed, feminism could not pretend that the world revolves around the struggle for parity between white women and white men.

Whiteness as the Standard

The worldview and experiences of white communities is also shaping the debate about identity politics. Racial identity is an invented series of social categories which have impacts on power and agency socially, economically, and politically. Though race is socially constructed, it has material and practical implications for the lives of those who have been assigned racial categories at the losing end of the spectrum of power. Racial categorizations that fall on the side of the spectrum that are non-white tend to lack power and agency vis-à-vis those that are on the white side of the spectrum.

Whiteness in America functions the same way that a "control" does in an experiment. In an experiment, to measure whether or not change has happened, you have to have a control—largely considered to be a standard against which change is compared. You know if change has occurred through your experiment when the entity being experimented on changes as a result of your intervention—because the control does not change.

In the social experiment called America, progress or change is determined by whether or not conditions have changed for white people and against a white standard.

What Are the Main Sources of Division in Contemporary America?

Another way to look at this is not as an experiment, but instead, through the lens of what is considered "normal." If I go to the store right now and look for Band-Aids, the color will be compatible with white skin, not mine. If I look for a pair of pantyhose, it's not as likely I'll find a shade that matches my skin. And up until a year ago, it was close to impossible for women of color to find shades of foundation. In America, "nude" or "flesh-toned" means white. Again, the standard in America is what is white—what appeals to white people, what makes sense to white people, what activates and motivates white people, and so on. It's not just true at the beauty store—it's true throughout the economy, our democracy, and the rest of our society.

If whiteness is the standard, it also is the criteria used to determine whether ideas, actions, or experiences have worth, merit, or value. Whiteness attempts to determine what is valid. Too often, whiteness dismisses the experiences and worldviews of people who are not white, because the opinions, values, needs, and beliefs of people who are not white are not considered to have merit, particularly when compared to whiteness.

When the Black Lives Matter movement exploded across the world, whiteness worked to define whether or not the anger of Black people was legitimate and justified, and at the same time, whiteness attempted to redefine the movement as dangerous, aimless, misguided, and violent. Whiteness attempted to de-fang the power of Black Lives Matter as a slogan and a rallying cry with "All Lives Matter" effectively erasing any mention of race. Changing "Black Lives Matter" to "All Lives Matter" turns what was a discourse on structural racism, police, and other forms of state violence into a two-dimensional conversation where race either does or doesn't matter. Race-neutral language is a core tenet of whiteness—race, and racial oppression or racial exclusion, is made invisible on the surface while at the same time being allowed to organize the economy, democracy, and society.

Whiteness is the control and the standard because whiteness is fundamentally about power. Whiteness attempts to shape worldviews, ideas, and experiences because whiteness seeks to maintain the power it has been afforded, and subsequently affords to people who have been designated as white, for the purposes of implementing whiteness and, as such, implementing power.

The debate over identity politics is no exception to this rule.

Not everyone sees identity politics as a gift. In the aftermath of the 2016 election, a plethora of articles appeared in news outlets, slamming "liberal identity politics." Television pundits began to decry "identity politics" as the reason that Democrats lost the presidential election.

There are a number of arguments that are deployed against identity politics, and they are deployed for a number of reasons. One such argument declares that a fixation on diversity renders people incapable of seeing outside of their own experience, preventing them from being able to build relationships with those who do not share their experiences. And, in the political realm, they argue that a focus on differences, rather than what we share in common, is a strategic mistake in elections. It is worth noting that these arguments are primarily deployed towards those who are not white.

These arguments rest on the notion that identity politics, as they define them, leave people out—and yet they fail to acknowledge that the politics of identity are not responsible for the prevalence of those identities. Identity is only important when—through no fault of your own—you are assigned an identity that promises worse life outcomes than those who are not assigned an identity that is marginalized from power.

Following the logic of contrarians of identity politics, no one should pay attention to the fact that being assigned "Black" almost guarantees that your life chances will be worse than someone who is assigned a "white" identity, because it could alienate a white person and leave them out of the conversation. Instead of addressing the fact that Black people are more likely to die in childbirth than white people, that Black people with disabilities are eight times more likely to be shot and killed by police than their white counterparts, that Black people on average are twice as likely to be poor or to be unemployed than white people, or that white households are 13 times as wealthy as Black households, critics of identity politics would prefer we not address these disparities, for fear of alienating people who are not experiencing them.

The real problem in America isn't identity politics and making difference visible—it's that those discrepancies exist in the first place.

Critics of identity politics, intentionally or unintentionally, uphold a logic of whiteness that functions in similar ways to that of the edict presented in the movie The Wizard of Oz—they want you to pay no attention to the man behind the curtain.

Does Identity Politics Bridge or Divide?

Another fallacy from critics of identity politics is that identifying and addressing differences somehow prevent people with different histories, backgrounds, ethnicities, identities, or experiences from finding commonality.

For example, Black communities are not the only ones who suffer from the ways in which whiteness distributes power unevenly in favor of white communities. Communities who are not white are not a monolith—and communities who share an experience of marginalization or disenfranchisement can and often do come together, across their differences, to end that marginalization. But this doesn't and shouldn't mean that they leave their identities at the door. Just like Black communities experience the negative effects of entrenched white power, so do Latinx communities, Arab communities, Muslim communities, Pacific Islander communities, Asian diasporic communities, and so on.

To be clear, these communities do not just come together because they are marginalized. They come together to achieve a common goal—freedom and equality for all of us.

Critics of identity politics are correct when they caution that a focus primarily on experience can detract from building alliances or developing a plan of action. That certainly is true when identity politics isn't geared towards shifting the balance of power. However, critics of identity politics should be careful not to paint with such a broad brush. The Combahee River Collective wasn't a knitting circle—they were a group of Black women, many of whom identified as lesbian and poor, who pushed the movements they should have been a part of to be more effective in acknowledging the impacts of race, class, gender, disability and more on the issues they were trying to impact, together, for the sake of the collective.

Demanding that anyone divorce their lived experience from their participation in political action is not only dangerous, but it serves to reinforce power dynamics that are bad for the collective.

What's ironic about the controversy surrounding identity politics is that few seem to take issue with the white identity politics shaping our lives. The critiques of identity politics only arise when those who are marginalized and disconnected from power assert that their experiences matter, and demand action to ensure that they can, in fact, achieve parity socially, economically, and politically with whites.

In the lead up to the 2016 Presidential election, Donald Trump ran on the slogan of "Make America Great Again." Making America great again insinuated that America was great before, leaving one to ask: "What are we trying to restore America to, and what are we trying to change it from?" Throughout the campaign, the answer became clear—America, apparently, was great before its demographics changed, before women had rights, before Black people could stand up for their rights, and so on. The America invoked by Trump was an America run and dominated by white, Christian, heterosexual men. That America was powered by blue-collar manufacturing jobs, and in that America, people of color, women, and others did not have equal rights to white men. In that America, the one that Trump and before him President Ronald Reagan idealized, it was illegal for Black people to share public accommodations with white people.

The problem that those who decried identity politics had, then, was with what identity politics did when used to empower those who lacked power—in society, in the economy, and in American democracy.

Identity politics is a threat to those who hold and wield power, because it destabilizes the control against which all else is compared. Identity politics is a threat to white power because it asserts that whiteness has shaped all of our lives in ways that do not benefit us—even those who possess that privilege. Far from being an edict of political correctness, identity politics asks us to see the world as it actually is, and more than that, it demands that we equalize the playing field.

Those who claim that identity politics is counterproductive and divisive often seek to build movements on that which they claim we all have in common, and cite economic status as an equalizer that everyone can get behind. Yet in an economy that is racialized and gendered, such notions are wishful thinking at best, and willful ignorance at worst.

The Consequences of a False Debate

The fight over identity politics is a false one; it forces false choices and even worse, inauthentic ones. Conservative movements have identified race and gender in particular as arenas where neutrality is strategic to maintain white, heterosexual, male, cisgendered power, at the expense of everyone who does not occupy those social positions. They have identified that inequality resulting from race and gender, and other social indicators that have economic implications, is best left undiscussed, lest it be uncovered that there are people that benefit from the disenfranchisement and oppression of marginalized communities. Simultaneously, the same forces inside of liberal and progressive movements have adopted the same stance, using talking points from conservatives to justify their resistance to upending oppressions other than that resulting from economic inequality.

This, of course, has consequences for progressive movements and civic engagement efforts. A refusal to acknowledge inequities inside of a movement almost guarantees that those inequities will politics/archive/2019/02/racial-divisions-exist-among-whites-blacks-and-hispanics/583267/.

Gary Younge, "'The United States Is Broken as Hell'—the Division in Politics over Race and Class," *Guardian*, September 9, 2019. https://www.theguardian.com/us-news/2019/sep/09/the-united-states-is-broken-as-hell-the-division-in-politics-over-race-and-class.

OPPOSING VIEWPOINTS® SERIES

CHAPTER 2

Has America Become More Divided over Time?

Chapter Preface

In the wake of the highly contentious U.S. presidential elections in 2016 and 2020, it is easy to assume that the American public is more divided than ever before. Combine this with the attack on the U.S. Capitol on January 6, 2021, in which a mob attempted to prevent Congress from formalizing the election of President Joe Biden, and it seems evident that tensions in America are at a boiling point. While studies indicate that polarization has indeed increased in recent decades, and acts of political violence like the January 6 attack do suggest the potential start of a troubling trend, experts are divided on whether the division America is currently facing is truly unprecedented.

America has always had a two-party, winner-takes all political system that pits one party and its supporters against the other. However, according to an article published by the American Political Science Association's Committee on Political Parties (APSA) in 1950, at that time the parties were relatively similar.[1] They did not have the strong coalitions of voters that characterize each party today, meaning the political parties were not as strongly associated with voters' social and ideological identities at that time. Additionally, this meant that bipartisanship—cooperation between the two parties in legislation—was more common. It has only been since 1969 that the issue of divided government—in which the president is from a different party than at least one of the bodies of Congress—has caused a large amount of fighting between the parties that has hindered legislation.[2]

Nonetheless, research indicates that America is not as divided as most Americans might think. According to research from the Carr Center, the significant majority of Americans tend to agree on key issues, such as the freedoms that define American identity and the rights that are essential to life in the U.S., including education, equality, healthcare, and clean air and water.[3] And while many Americans worry that the intense division in American politics will lead to more political violence and possibly even a new civil war, according to research from Citizen Data, 85 percent of Americans from both political parties believe violence is rarely or never acceptable in politics.[4]

The viewpoints in this chapter examine data and events from America's history to consider how the issue of division has evolved over time. They examine both the role division plays in the structure of American politics and the values that unite Americans in spite of these tensions.

Notes

1. "Political Parties: What is divided government?" Lumen Learning. https://courses.lumenlearning.com/americangovernment/chapter/divided-government-and-partisan-polarization/.
2. *Ibid.*
3. Shawn Griffiths, "America Is Not as Divided as The Parties Want You to Think," IVN Network, February 19, 2021.https://ivn.us/posts/america-is-not-as-divided-as-the-parties-want-you-to-think.
4. *Ibid.*

VIEWPOINT 1

| *"Divided government can pose considerable difficulties for both the operations of the party and the government as a whole."*

Division in American Politics Is Not New

Lumen Learning

According to this excerpted viewpoint by Lumen Learning, division in U.S. politics has not always been an issue, but it also isn't a problem that has arisen in recent years. A divided government, in which the president's political party differs from the majority party in at least one branch of Congress, has been common in the U.S. since 1969. However, in the early years of this pattern, bipartisan cooperation between politicians in both parties was much more common. It is only in recent decades that polarization and a lack of cooperation between the parties has become a major issue. This polarization makes it more difficult for the government to operate effectively and excludes political moderates from the political process. Lumen Learning is a website that offers free, open-source course materials.

As you read, consider the following questions:

1. According to the 1950 report by APSA cited in this viewpoint, was political polarization an issue in American politics at that time?

"Political Parties: What is divided government?" Lumen Learning. https://courses.lumenlearning.com/americangovernment/chapter/divided-government-and-partisan-polarization/. Licensed under CC BY 4.0 International.

2. What example does the author provide of the threat divided government causes to government operations?
3. What effect has polarization had on the participation of moderates in party politics, according to this viewpoint?

In 1950, the American Political Science Association's Committee on Political Parties (APSA) published an article offering a criticism of the current party system. The parties, it argued, were too similar. Distinct, cohesive political parties were critical for any well-functioning democracy. First, distinct parties offer voters clear policy choices at election time. Second, cohesive parties could deliver on their agenda, even under conditions of lower bipartisanship. The party that lost the election was also important to democracy because it served as the "loyal opposition" that could keep a check on the excesses of the party in power. Finally, the paper suggested that voters could signal whether they preferred the vision of the current leadership or of the opposition. This signaling would keep both parties accountable to the people and lead to a more effective government, better capable of meeting the country's needs.

But, the APSA article continued, U.S. political parties of the day were lacking in this regard. Rarely did they offer clear and distinct visions of the country's future, and, on the rare occasions they did, they were typically unable to enact major reforms once elected. Indeed, there was so much overlap between the parties when in office that it was difficult for voters to know whom they should hold accountable for bad results. The article concluded by advocating a set of reforms that, if implemented, would lead to more distinct parties and better government. While this description of the major parties as being too similar may have been accurate in the 1950s; that is no longer the case.[1]

The Problem of Divided Government

The problem of majority versus minority politics is particularly acute under conditions of divided government. Divided government occurs when one or more houses of the legislature are controlled by the party in opposition to the executive. Unified government occurs when the same party controls the executive and the legislature entirely. Divided government can pose considerable difficulties for both the operations of the party and the government as a whole. It makes fulfilling campaign promises extremely difficult, for instance, since the cooperation (or at least the agreement) of both Congress and the president is typically needed to pass legislation. Furthermore, one party can hardly claim credit for success when the other side has been a credible partner, or when nothing can be accomplished. Party loyalty may be challenged too, because individual politicians might be forced to oppose their own party agenda if it will help their personal reelection bids.

Divided government can also be a threat to government operations, although its full impact remains unclear.[2] For example, when the divide between the parties is too great, government may shut down. A 1976 dispute between Republican president Gerald Ford and a Democrat-controlled Congress over the issue of funding for certain cabinet departments led to a ten-day shutdown of the government (although the federal government did not cease to function entirely). But beginning in the 1980s, the interpretation that Republican president Ronald Reagan's attorney general gave to a nineteenth-century law required a complete shutdown of federal government operations until a funding issue was resolved.[3]

Clearly, the parties' willingness to work together and compromise can be a very good thing. However, the past several decades have brought an increased prevalence of divided government. Since 1969, the U.S. electorate has sent the president a Congress of his own party in only seven of twenty-three congressional elections, and during George W. Bush's first administration, the Republican majority was so narrow that a combination of resignations and defections gave the Democrats control before the next election could be held.

Over the short term, however, divided government can make for very contentious politics. A well-functioning government usually requires a certain level of responsiveness on the part of both the executive and the legislative branches. This responsiveness is hard enough if government is unified under one party. During the presidency of Democrat Jimmy Carter (1977–1980), despite the fact that both houses of Congress were controlled by Democratic majorities, the government was shut down on five occasions because of conflict between the executive and legislative branches.[4]

Shutdowns are even more likely when the president and at least one house of Congress are of opposite parties. During the presidency of Ronald Reagan, for example, the federal government shut down eight times; on seven of those occasions, the shutdown was caused by disagreements between Reagan and the Republican-controlled Senate on the one hand and the Democrats in the House on the other, over such issues as spending cuts, abortion rights, and civil rights.[5] More such disputes and government shutdowns took place during the administrations of George H. W. Bush, Bill Clinton, and Barack Obama, when different parties controlled Congress and the presidency.

For the first few decades of the current pattern of divided government, the threat it posed to the government appears to have been muted by a high degree of bipartisanship, or cooperation through compromise. Many pieces of legislation were passed in the 1960s and 1970s with reasonably high levels of support from both parties. Most members of Congress had relatively moderate voting records, with regional differences within parties that made bipartisanship on many issues more likely.

For example, until the 1980s, northern and midwestern Republicans were often fairly progressive, supporting racial equality, workers' rights, and farm subsidies. Southern Democrats were frequently quite socially and racially conservative and were

Great Recession of 2008 and its assistance to endangered financial institutions, provided through the Troubled Asset Relief Program, TARP. The Occupy Movement believed government moved swiftly to protect the banking industry from the worst of the recession but largely failed to protect the average person, thereby worsening the growing economic inequality in the United States.

While the Occupy Movement itself has largely fizzled, the anti-business sentiment to which it gave voice continues within the Democratic Party, and many Democrats have proclaimed their support for the movement and its ideals, if not for its tactics.[10] Bernie Sanders' presidential run made these topics and causes even more salient, especially among younger voters. To date, however, the Occupy Movement has had fewer electoral effects than has the Tea Party. Yet, as manifested in Sanders' candidacy, it has the potential to affect races at lower levels in the 2016 national elections.

The Causes of Polarization

Scholars agree that some degree of polarization is occurring in the United States, even if some contend it is only at the elite level. But they are less certain about exactly why, or how, polarization has become such a mainstay of American politics. Several conflicting theories have been offered. The first and perhaps best argument is that polarization is a party-in-government phenomenon driven by a decades-long sorting of the voting public, or a change in party allegiance in response to shifts in party position.[11] According to the sorting thesis, before the 1950s, voters were mostly concerned with state-level party positions rather than national party concerns. Since parties are bottom-up institutions, this meant local issues dominated elections; it also meant national-level politicians typically paid more attention to local problems than to national party politics.

But over the past several decades, voters have started identifying more with national-level party politics, and they began to demand their elected representatives become more attentive to national party positions. As a result, they have become more likely to pick parties that consistently represent national ideals, are more consistent in their candidate selection, and are more willing to elect office-holders likely to follow their party's national agenda. One example of the way social change led to party sorting revolves around race.

A second possible culprit in increased polarization is the impact of technology on the public square. Before the 1950s, most people got their news from regional newspapers and local radio stations. While some national programming did exist, most editorial control was in the hands of local publishers and editorial boards. These groups served as a filter of sorts as they tried to meet the demands of local markets.

Television was a powerful tool, with national news and editorial content that provided the same message across the country. All viewers saw the same images of the women's rights movement and the war in Vietnam. The expansion of news coverage to cable, and the consolidation of local news providers into big corporate conglomerates, amplified this nationalization. Average citizens were just as likely to learn what it meant to be a Republican from a politician in another state as from one in their own, and national news coverage made it much more difficult for politicians to run away from their votes. The information explosion that followed the heyday of network TV by way of cable, the Internet, and blogs has furthered this nationalization trend.

A final possible cause for polarization is the increasing sophistication of gerrymandering, or the manipulation of legislative districts in an attempt to favor a particular candidate. According to the gerrymandering thesis, the more moderate or heterogeneous a voting district, the more moderate the politician's behavior once in office. Taking extreme or one-sided positions on a large number of issues would be hazardous for a member who needs to build a diverse electoral coalition. But if the district has been drawn to favor a particular group, it now is necessary for the elected official to serve only the portion of the constituency that dominates.

Gerrymandering is a centuries-old practice. There has always been an incentive for legislative bodies to draw districts in such a way that sitting legislators have the best chance of keeping their jobs. But changes in law and technology have transformed gerrymandering from a crude art into a science. The first advance came with the introduction of the "one-person-one-vote" principle by the U.S. Supreme Court in 1962. Before then, it was common for many states to practice redistricting, or redrawing of their electoral maps, only if they gained or lost seats in the U.S. House of Representatives. This can happen once every ten years as a result of a constitutionally mandated reapportionment process, in which the number of House seats given to each state is adjusted to account for population changes.

But if there was no change in the number of seats, there was little incentive to shift district boundaries. After all, if a legislator had won election based on the current map, any change to the map could make losing seats more likely. Even when reapportionment led to new maps, most legislators were more concerned with protecting their own seats than with increasing the number of seats held by their party. As a result, some districts had gone decades without significant adjustment, even as the U.S. population changed from largely rural to largely urban. By the early 1960s, some electoral districts had populations several times greater than those of their more rural neighbors.

However, in its one-person-one-vote decision in *Reynolds v. Simms* (1964), the Supreme Court argued that everyone's vote should count roughly the same regardless of where they lived. [12] Districts had to be adjusted so they would have roughly equal populations. Several states therefore had to make dramatic changes to their electoral maps during the next two redistricting cycles (1970–1972 and 1980–1982). Map designers, no longer certain how to protect individual party members, changed tactics to try and create safe seats so members of their party could be assured of winning by a comfortable margin. The basic rule of thumb was that designers sought to draw districts in which their preferred party had a 55 percent or better chance of winning a given district, regardless of which candidate the party nominated.

Of course, many early efforts at post-Reynolds gerrymandering were crude since map designers had no good way of knowing exactly where partisans lived. At best, designers might have a rough idea of voting patterns between precincts, but they lacked the ability to know voting patterns in individual blocks or neighborhoods. They also had to contend with the inherent mobility of the U.S. population, which meant the most carefully drawn maps could be obsolete just a few years later. Designers were often forced to use crude proxies for party, such as race or the socio-economic status of a neighborhood. Some maps were so crude they were ruled unconstitutionally discriminatory by the courts.

Proponents of the gerrymandering thesis point out that the decline in the number of moderate voters began during this period of increased redistricting. But it was not until later, they argue, that the real effects could be seen. A second advance in redistricting, via computer-aided map making, truly transformed gerrymandering into a science. Refined computing technology, the ability to collect data about potential voters, and the use of advanced algorithms have given map makers a good deal of certainty about where to place district boundaries to best predetermine the outcomes. These factors also provided better predictions about future population shifts, making the effects of gerrymandering more stable over time. Proponents argue that this increased efficiency in map drawing has led to the disappearance of moderates in Congress.

According to political scientist Nolan McCarty, there is little evidence to support the redistricting hypothesis alone. First, he argues, the Senate has become polarized just as the House of Representatives has, but people vote for Senators on a statewide basis. There are no gerrymandered voting districts in elections for senators. Research showing that more partisan candidates first win election to the House before then running successfully for the Senate, however, helps us understand how the Senate can also become partisan.[13] Furthermore, states like Wyoming and

Vermont, which have only one Representative and thus elect House members on a statewide basis as well, have consistently elected people at the far ends of the ideological spectrum.[14] Redistricting did contribute to polarization in the House of Representatives, but it took place largely in districts that had undergone significant change.[15]

Furthermore, polarization has been occurring throughout the country, but the use of increasingly polarized district design has not. While some states have seen an increase in these practices, many states were already largely dominated by a single party (such as in the Solid South) but still elected moderate representatives. Some parts of the country have remained closely divided between the two parties, making overt attempts at gerrymandering difficult. But when coupled with the sorting phenomenon discussed above, redistricting probably is contributing to polarization, if only at the margins.

[…]

Notes

1. Nolan "McCarty, Keith T. Poole and Howard Rosenthal. 2006. *Polarized America*. Cambridge, MA: MIT Press."
2. David "R. Mayhew. 1991. *Divided We Govern*. New Haven: Yale University Press; George C. Edwards, Andrew Barrett and Jeffrey S. Peake, "The Legislative Impact of Divided Government," American Journal of Political Science 41, no. 2 (1997): 545–563."
3. Dylan "Matthews, "Here is Every Previous Government Shutdown, Why They Happened and How They Ended," The *Washington Post*, 25 September 2013."
4. Matthews, ""Here is Every Previous Government Shutdown, Why They Happened and How They Ended.""
5. Matthews, ""Here is Every Previous Government Shutdown, Why They Happened and How They Ended.""
6. Drew "Desilver, "The Polarized Congress of Today Has Its Roots in the 1970s," 12 June 2014, http://www.pewresearch.org/fact-tank/2014/06/12/polarized-politics-in-congress-began-in-the-1970s-and-has-been-getting-worse-ever-since/ (March 16, 2016)."
7. "The "Tea Party and Religion," 23 February 2011, http://www.pewforum.org/2011/02/23/tea-party-and-religion/ (March 16, 2016)."
8. "The "Tea Party and Religion.""
9. Paul "Waldman, "Nearly All the GOP Candidates Bow Down to Grover Norquist, The *Washington Post,* 13 August 2015, https://www.washingtonpost.com/blogs/plum-line/wp/2015/08/13/nearly-all-the-gop-candidates-bow-down-to-grover-norquist/ (March 1, 2016)."

10. Beth "Fouhy, "Occupy Wall Street and Democrats Remain Wary of Each Other," *Huffington Post*, 17 November 2011."
11. Morris "Fiorina, "Americans Have Not Become More Politically Polarized," The *Washington Post,* 23 June 2014."
12. *Reynolds v. Simms*, 379 U.S. 870 (1964).
13. Sean "Theriault. 2013. *The Gingrich Senators: The Roots of Partisan Warfare in Congress.* New York: Oxford University Press."
14. Nolan "McCarty, "Hate Our Polarized Politics? Why You Can't Blame Gerrymandering," The *Washington Post*, 26 October 2012."
15. Jamie "L. Carson et al., "Redistricting and Party Polarization in the U.S. House of Representatives," *American Politics Research* 35, no. 6 (2007): 878–904."

Viewpoint 2

> *"Most Americans, across the political spectrum, do not condone violent behavior in the pursuit of a cause— or at the very least think it is rarely a right course of action."*

Though the Government Is Divided, Americans Today Are Not Nearly as Divided as They Seem

Shawn Griffiths

In this viewpoint, Shawn Griffiths asserts that although America seems very divided today, that is because it benefits politicians and political parties to create this image of division, in which there are two distinct teams that are completely opposed to one another. However, data from multiple recent surveys does not back up the assertion that the American public is highly ideologically divided. The press also plays a role in creating this image of a divided America. In reality, most voters from both parties agree on many key issues, most Americans believe that politics should never turn violent, and many Americans believe they have a lot in common with Americans of any political affiliation. Shawn Griffiths is an election reform expert and national editor of Independent Voter News.

"America Is Not as Divided as The Parties Want You to Think," by Shawn Griffiths, IVN Network, February 19, 2021. Reprinted by permission.

Has America Become More Divided over Time?

As you read, consider the following questions:

1. According to the Citizen Data survey referenced in this viewpoint, what percentage of Americans view violence as rarely or never acceptable for holding people in power accountable?
2. What percentage of Black Lives Matter (BLM) protests were peaceful, according to this viewpoint?
3. According to the data from the Carr Center referenced in this viewpoint, what share of Americans think Americans have more in common with each other than they tend to believe?

The United States has never seemed more divided. The political landscape seems like a perpetual powder keg—one spark will ignite the flames and consume the nation. Some have even suggested that the country could be on the verge of another civil war.

This is, at least, how the press and the major players of the political process want people to view America. But are the people of the United States really this divided? Are we really a breath away from chaos across the country?

The short answer: No.

Party Division Is Hurting Our Country, and Our Politics, but It Does Not Represent the Public

It is true that the parties are more divided today than at any other point in modern U.S. history. A Pew Research study dating back to 2014 found that in the previous 20 years, there was gradually less and less overlap between the Republican and Democratic parties.

"And a new survey of 10,000 adults nationwide finds that these divisions are greatest among those who are the most engaged and active in the political process," Pew said in the report.

But the expanding divide between the two parties does not extend to all of America. The parties would like people to think so, because they control the levers of government and at the end of the day, the narrative in the press sums everything up in terms of "Team Red" vs "Team Blue."

Many Republicans and many Democrats, both in the media and on the campaign trail, talk about the opposing party like they are existential threats to the country. As a result, polling shows that many who identify with both parties view the "other side" as enemies, rather than just "political opponents."

This is the result of an electoral system that has become solely about the us-versus-them struggle between the parties. It's a win-at-all cost environment, in which the stakes rise in perpetuity—and so what both sides are willing to say or do to win rises in perpetuity as well.

What we see on the campaign trail is no longer merely a political contest between the parties—it is partisan warfare. There is a proverbial call-to-arms against the other side as the fate of the nation hangs in the balance. If the wrong side wins, the nation as we know it is doomed.

I wrote about this in 2018 in the wake of the Brett Kavanaugh confirmation process. Policymakers then were threatened with violence and death, envelopes filled with suspicious substances were sent to administration officials, and Senate Republicans were doxxed.

Consider the state of the campaign narrative then:

While in office and on the campaign trail, former President Trump repeatedly said that Democrats will turn the United States into Venezuela and crime will run rampant as illegal aliens pour into the country unchecked. Other Republicans running for office made similar assertions.

Meanwhile, in November 2018, Hillary Clinton said her party cannot be civil with Republicans who want to destroy Democratic values unless the party won back the House or took the Senate, and Eric Holder said, "When they (Republicans) go low, we kick them!"

The language hasn't improved in the last couple of years. In fact, it continues to get worse as policymakers post on social media and send emails claiming the "other side" is a threat—not just wrong or the wrong choice—but a threat to the nation.

The most hateful and vitriolic political messages voters can find are on social media sites like Facebook and Twitter, and within these mediums exist echo chambers used to enforce a deeply held bias by those who have chosen a side between "Team Red" and "Team Blue." But, not only are these echo chambers—which in truth are not that large, but are extremely condensed—used to vindicate an already held belief, but also to inflame passions and spur hate that feeds on itself in a vicious cycle.

The press also runs with the rhetoric, framing a narrative that the country is hotly divided in what might as well amount to a spectator sport. Yet, many pundits and commentators do not ask what impact it could have on individuals with a greater inclination toward violence or destruction.

Keep in mind, to many who have chosen a side, this is not just a political competition between two sides with opposing ideas. This is a partisan war where one side is always right and good, which by contrast means the other side has to always be wrong and evil.

What will the most radicalized segments of society do to win a partisan war Republicans and Democrats say they must win to preserve the future of America? What length would they go to, in their minds, defeat evil?

To cause great harm, it doesn't take many.

Yet, the stakes only get more dire each election cycle. The rhetoric only gets more divisive, and in the seven years since Pew's research, the divide between the Republican and Democratic Parties has only become more pronounced—and damaging to the constitutional republic.

The "spirit of party," as George Washington once called it and warned, has become a flame that consumes, rather than warms.

Washington's farewell address is well known, yet his warning about political factions has long been ignored, yet our first and only independent president's words proved to be as prophetic as Alexis de Toqueville's:

[The spirit of party] agitates the community with ill-founded jealousies and false alarms, kindles the animosity of one part against another, foments occasionally riot and insurrection. It opens the door to foreign influence and corruption, which finds a facilitated access to the government itself through the channels of party passions. Thus the policy and the will of one country are subjected to the policy and will of another.

This is not to say there is no room for parties, but we are seeing the unintended consequences of a system where two parties are the sole gatekeepers of our elections, and foster greater division in the pursuit of maintaining and growing political power.

Due to the fact that elections and the nation's politics is solely about "Team Red" and "Team Blue," the narrative suggests this growing divide represents America as a whole. Yet, this is a fallacy and must be called out.

Those who stormed the U.S. Capitol on January 6, for instance, do not account for a statistically relevant percentage of the population. They don't even represent a majority of Trump voters, or those who believe the election results were illegitimate.

Consider this:

Citizen Data reports that 85 percent of Americans surveyed believe that violence is "never" or "rarely" justified in the pursuit of holding those in power accountable, Among those who felt the presidential election results were illegitimate, 82 percent said violence is "never" or "rarely" justified.

Similarly, while some on the right point to upheaval during BLM protests in 2020 as an example of violence on the left, a report showed that 93 percent of protests were peaceful—which does not get into the nuances of who instigated or escalated non-peaceful actions.

And, the percentage of respondents in the Citizen Data report who said violence, looting and rioting were "not very" or "not at all" justifiable when it came to both the protests against racial injustice and the attack on the U.S. Capitol reached levels of 88 percent or higher.

This means that most Americans, across the political spectrum, do not condone violent behavior in the pursuit of a cause—or at the very least think it is rarely a right course of action. Does this sound like a country on the brink?

This is not to say that violence, rioting, destruction of property, and actions that threaten the safety of others should not be condemned or prosecuted. It does, however, speak to how much the minority has been used to represent the whole of a group in a partisan-driven narrative.

Also consider that most Americans want to see lawmakers work together. In a January 2019 NPR/PBS/Marist Poll, 63 percent of U.S. adults surveyed said the statement, "I like elected officials who make compromises with people they disagree with," is close to their views.

It seems consistent with other polls that a little over a third of the electorate are staunch partisans. They reject compromise, and they want their public officials to stick to a party or ideological line, no matter what.

Yet, despite representing a political minority, these voters win out with elected public officials because of the outsized power they have in elections. Thus, the prevailing narrative is that the country is hotly divided on everything, even when that narrative is a manufactured lie.

Remember what I said about the damaging effect the narrative on social media is having? If a person spends most of their time online following only people who report and commentate on politics, it might seem like the partisan hatefest online is much more prevalent than it is.

However, Pew Research found in 2019 that only 22 percent of U.S. adults use Twitter, which is a platform that has received a great deal of attention since Donald Trump launched his presidential campaign in 2015. Not even 1-in-4 adults use it though.

And, of the 22 percent of U.S. adults that use Twitter, only 13 percent of their public tweets are about national politics, and 97 percent of those tweets are from the most active 10 percent of users.

Consider this information for a moment because it further speaks to how the political system allows a marginal percentage of Americans to have the most seats at the table.

The U.S.'s Two-Party Political Narrative Is Vastly Devoid of Understanding

It isn't just on the subject of compromise that voters largely agree. A report released in August 2020 based on more than 30 in-depth surveys conducted by the University of Maryland's Program for Public Consultation identified nearly 150 key policy positions on which majorities in both parties agree.

These policy positions cover the broad scope of the nation's most important and seemingly contentious issues, including trade, immigration, police reform, jobs, social security, budget, taxes, energy and the environment, and many more.

What is important to note about the surveys conducted, which gathered responses from over 80,000 Americans, is that when both sides of an issue are laid out, explained in-depth, and proposed solutions evaluated, voters tend to gravitate toward common interests and goals.

"What's striking is that when citizens think through the issues and hear both sides, they often find common ground—clearly, much more so than Members of Congress," said Steven Kull, director of the Program for Public Consultation.

Read that again: "When citizens think through the issues and hear both sides, they often find common ground."

This is something the mainstream political narrative is severely lacking. Where voters consume their news often favors only one side, and the conversation on the campaign trail and the press lack the necessary nuances and substance to foster understanding.

U.S. elections are not about understanding. They are not about substance. They are not about bringing voters together. They are about tearing voters apart. They are about "Team Red" and "Team Blue." There is no room for common ground when all that matters is who wins.

This has even impacted how polling is conducted. Voters are expected to identify with one side or the other, and issues are not presented in a comprehensive manner. Many times, questions are phrased a certain way to get a desired result.

However, the Program for Public Consultation isn't the only group that has reported on the broad agreement among Americans. Harvard's Carr Center found in September 2020 that 7 in 10 Americans believe they have more in common with one another than people think.

Note: this is when elections are the most divisive. And yet, even during the campaign sprint to Election Day, most voters held on to the belief that they were not as divided as the national political narrative would suggest.

"Overall I think Americans want not to be divided as politics are forcing it to be, and that's probably the biggest message of this poll," said John Shattuck, as quoted by Politico. Shattuck is the director of the Carr Center's project on Reimagining Rights and Responsibilities in the United States. He is also a former U.S. assistant secretary of State of Democracy, Human Rights, and Labor.

"Division is not what most Americans are seeking."

Specifically, the Carr Center poll looked at the subject of rights and freedoms, including those not explicitly guaranteed in the U.S. Constitution. Overall, 8 in 10 Americans surveyed agreed with the statement, "without our freedoms America is nothing." Here are some notable findings from the poll:

- 93 percent of individuals surveyed considered the right to clean air and water essential;
- Similarly, 93 percent said the right to protected privacy was important;
- 92 percent said the same about the right to a quality education;
- 92 percent said the same about racial equality;
- 89 percent said the same about affordable health care; and
- 85 percent said the same about the right to a job

Getting deeper into the weeds, there will be more disagreement on how we approach these rights, but there is clearly a foundation from which to find common ground and understanding. From understanding comes empathy which fosters a desire to find mutually beneficial solutions.

Business Insider reported on just some of the issues and values that continue to unite Americans in 2017, based on reports from Pew Research, Gallup, and the General Social Survey run by the NORC at the University of Chicago. The analysis was broken down by topic.

On the subject of democracy, for instance, *Business Insider* looked at findings from Pew Research that found that nearly all Americans believe in the importance of

- Fair and open elections;
- A system of checks and balances;
- The right to nonviolent protests;
- Protecting the rights of individuals with unpopular opinions; and
- The freedom of news organizations to criticize political leaders.

Business Insider also used Pew Research to examine where Americans overwhelmingly agree on federal taxes, immigration, health care and paid leave from work, and other areas. It further used the General Social Survey to examine what unites Americans on the subject of federal funding for improving the environment, education, infrastructure, and mass transit, and used Gallup to examine where Americans agreed on then-President Donald Trump's campaign promises.

And, this just scratches the surface of the available data that shows critical areas of common ground among voters, and when there isn't clear common ground, there is a willingness and a desire to seek it out and to work with the people with different views.

Beginning this conversation simply requires a starting point of mutual agreement. It begins with nearly everyone agreeing to a basic concept and from there we can build ladders that extend to substantive solutions that are mutually beneficial to a greater number of people.

And here lies the problem. The political landscape is governed by an electoral process designed to limit competition, which means reducing the need to compete for the most voters possible and limits the marketplace of ideas which denies a more nuanced dialogue.

The U.S. political system, as I have discussed, instead amplifies division between two points of view, forcing people to pick a side, and by doing so feeds into people's confirmation bias and conditions people to adopt a mindset of contrasts:

My side always has to be right; the other side has to always be wrong. My side is good; the other side is evil. My side will save America; the other side will destroy it.

It might be hard to believe, but unless broad systemic changes are adopted things will only escalate in future election cycles—because this mindset can only send the political narrative in a downward spiral.

The only way to prevent this to provide an equal, fair, and accountable playing field for candidates and voters so that competition can emerge, and not just competition of candidates, but competition of ideas.

We have already established that a starting point of mutual agreement is that nearly all voters believe in the importance of free, fair, and open elections. Yet, many Americans also agree that the U.S political system right now is failing to provide that. We have a system of zero accountability, zero empathy, and zero leadership.

Changing this begins with changing the means by which we elect our leaders. We have a system that forces voters to come to the parties, which has created the zero sum elections we have. We need to create a system that forces the parties, and their candidates, to go to voters.

It would lead to greater accountability, which would in turn foster greater empathy as public officials would have to really listen to the concerns of voters, and from that real leaders can emerge to tackle the nation's biggest issues in a comprehensive and nuanced way.

VIEWPOINT 3

"Once you engage in political violence, it becomes easier to do it again. But if there's an effective state response to these events, then it can help strengthen those institutions."

Political Violence Could Be on the Rise in America

Naomi Schalit and Ore Koren

This viewpoint features an interview between Naomi Schalit and Ore Koren on political violence in the wake of the attack of the U.S. Capitol on January 6, 2021. In many ways, the U.S. is different from countries where political violence is common, which made the attack shocking. More often political violence occurs in places with weak democratic institutions and economies, where the state has little power to prevent violent attacks. Once there is a precedent of political violence, however, it becomes more likely that it will occur again. That is why a strong response to these actions plays an important role in maintaining the stability of a country. Naomi Schalit is the politics and society senior editor for the Conversation. *Ore Koren is an assistant professor of political science at Indiana University.*

"'Once You Engage in Political Violence, It Becomes Easier to Do It Again'—An Expert on Political Violence Reflects on Events at the Capitol," by Naomi Schalit and Ore Koren, The Conversation, January 7, 2021. https://theconversation.com/once-you-engage-in-political-violence-it-becomes-easier-to-do-it-again-an-expert-on-political-violence-reflects-on-events-at-the-capitol-152801. Licensed under CC BY 4.0 International.

As you read, consider the following questions:

1. According to Ore Koren, what is the difference between the U.S. and other countries with advanced economies and militaries where political violence occurs?
2. What does Koren offer as an example of an effective response to political violence?
3. What does Koren consider to be a major cause of the attack on the Capitol?

Editor's note: Ore Koren is a scholar of civil conflict and political violence. Before the November 2020 election, he wrote a story for The Conversation *about the likelihood of election-related violence in the U.S. So we went back to him on Wednesday, while what some are calling an insurrection unfolded at the U.S. Capitol, to ask him for some perspective on the event. This transcript has been edited for length and clarity.*

Q: You're a scholar of political violence. What were you thinking as you watched what's happened at the U.S. Capitol?

Koren: First of all, I felt pretty stunned. I think that's a natural response to this. This is a new situation; it shows the power of misinformation and stuff that we're not really good at dealing with.

My research focuses on organized political violence, which often happens in places where the state does not have much power to prevent violence, where the economy is underdeveloped, where democratic institutions are weak, and where there is a history of organized violence. And usually when we see events at this magnitude, they are accompanied by many casualties, which thankfully was not the case today.

What happened at the Capitol, from what I can tell, was a messy riot where people lashed out at the heart of American democracy, but it remains unclear how organized an effort this was.

AMERICA HAS NOT BEEN THIS DIVIDED SINCE THE CIVIL WAR

Political analyst Bill Schneider on Wednesday said the political environment in the U.S. is the most divided since the Civil War.

"Nothing is ever permanent, but we are broken," Schneider, a professor of policy, government and international affairs at George Mason University, told Hill.TV's Joe Concha on "What America's Thinking."

"I'd say this is the most divided we've been since the Civil War," he added.

Schneider's comments come as polling indicates a divided electorate heading into November's midterm elections.

The controversy surrounding the sexual misconduct allegations against Supreme Court nominee Brett Kavanaugh has revealed a deep partisan divide, with most Republicans supporting Kavanaugh and a similar amount of Democrats opposing him.

A recent Politico/Morning Consult survey found that 70 percent of Democrats oppose his nomination, while 73 percent of Republicans back it.

Emily Ekins, polling director at the Cato Institute, said that while the country appears divided now, that doesn't mean it will necessarily stay that way for a long time.

"I think things can change pretty quickly," she said. "I mean, I think people thought the Republican Party was done after Richard Nixon, and here comes along Ronald Reagan just a few years later."

"Analyst Says US Is Most Divided Since Civil War," by Julia Manchester, The Hill, March 10, 2018.

What hugely contributed to all of this is misinformation. People mobilized based on a conspiracy with no evidence. I think this is a major problem that has to be addressed—I don't know how. But it is really crucial to address the underlying problem—that people believe in what they feel is real, not what is real.

Once you engage in political violence, it becomes easier to do it again. But if there's an effective state response to these events, then it can help strengthen those institutions.

So, I think a lot of people will be saying, look, this is all going to have long-term negative implications. But there's also a possibility that this can actually help in the long run by showing the grave consequences of manipulating democratic institutions for political gain. Again, it depends on how the state and politicians and security and everybody responds to this. But having a history of political violence is a pretty strong predictor of future violence.

I think it's really important for federal authorities to show their ability to tackle this. When it comes down to it, the government must show that it can protect American democracy, through force if necessary.

far fewer (12 percent) express that they have "a lot" of trust in the information that comes from national news organizations.

Americans tend to have greater trust in local news organizations—though there is somewhat of a decline here as well. A large majority of Americans (75 percent) still say they have at least some trust in the information that comes from local news organizations, modestly lower than the shares who said the same in 2016 (82 percent) and in late 2019 (79 percent). And again, far fewer express the highest level of trust (18 percent).

A similar partisan divide emerges when it comes to local news, though to a lesser extent. As of June 2021, Democrats are 18 percentage points more likely than Republicans to have at least some trust in the information that comes from local news organizations (84 percent vs. 66 percent, respectively)—a gap that is again larger than at any time in recent years. Five years ago, 85 percent of Democrats had at least some trust in local news organizations, while 79 percent of Republicans did.

Social media continues to engender a much lower level of trust. About a quarter of Americans (27 percent) say they have at least some trust in the information that comes from social networking sites, with just 4 percent expressing that they have a lot of trust in it. This is about on par with late 2019 when 26 percent said they had at least some trust, but somewhat lower than the 34 percent who said the same in 2016. (In 2016, this question was asked of internet-using U.S. adults.)

Social media is trusted by a minority of both parties, though a partisan gap still exists. About a third of Democrats and Democratic-leaning independents (34 percent) and 19 percent of Republicans and Republican leaners say they have at least some trust in the information that comes from social media—a 15-point gap. This gap is larger than gaps from any other time in recent years and has nearly doubled since late 2019.

VIEWPOINT 5

> *"Our results highlight another point about partisanship in contemporary society: It has become an important social identity. It extends beyond particular policy beliefs or support for specific politicians."*

Partisanship Has Become Part of Social Identity in America

Christopher McConnell, Yotam Margalit, Neil Malhotra, and Matthew Levendusky

According to this viewpoint, politics has not always been as contentious and emotional as it is today. Today, it affects how people interact with their family, friends, and coworkers. It is a source of many arguments and negative emotions, which is referred to as affective polarization. Affective polarization also impacts one's economic behavior. Politically motivated boycotts of companies have become increasingly common, and people are willing to do things that are less economically advantageous if they align with their partisan identity. Christopher McConnell is a PhD student at the Stanford Graduate School of Business, where Neil Malhotra is a professor of political economy. Yotam Margalit is an associate professor of political science at Tel Aviv University. Matthew Levendusky is an associate professor of political science at the University of Pennsylvania.

"Polarization Is Changing How Americans Work and Shop," by Christopher McConnell, Yotam Margalit, Neil Malhotra, and Matthew Levendusky, Harvard Business Review, May 19, 2017. Reprinted by permission.

As you read, consider the following questions:

1. What fraction of Democrats would be upset if their child married someone of the opposing political party, according to this viewpoint?
2. What are some of the examples of politically motivated boycotts referenced in this viewpoint?
3. What do the results of the four experiments the authors completed suggest about how partisanship affects economic behavior?

After the bruising and contentious 2016 U.S. presidential election, it's not surprising that Americans' evaluations of members of the opposite political party have reached an all-time low. According to data from the Pew Research Center, 45 percent of Republicans and 41 percent of Democrats think the other party is so dangerous that it is a threat to the health of the nation. This animus has spilled over into social networks: According to a HuffPost/YouGov poll, nearly half of Americans got into an argument with someone (a friend, family member, coworker, etc.) about the election last year. Fifty years ago few people expressed any anger when asked how they would feel if their child married someone from the other party. Today, one-third of Democrats and nearly half of Republicans would be deeply upset. On item after item, Americans not only disagree on the issues but also increasingly personally dislike those from the other party.

This is a phenomenon scholars call affective polarization. Political scientists have attributed a number of important consequences to the increase of affective polarization in the United States, chief among them increased gridlock and dysfunction in Washington, DC. But much less is known about whether affective polarization changes how we interact outside of politics. Do these partisan sentiments affect economic exchanges between individuals from opposing parties?

This question is especially timely given recent, post-election discussions of American consumers either supporting or boycotting companies for their association with the opposing party. For example, the group Grab Your Wallet has suggested that people boycott several companies over their ties to the Trump administration, including L.L. Bean and Macy's, and the #DeleteUber hashtag spread after Uber failed to support New York taxi drivers' protest of the administration's travel ban. Ivanka Trump's brand has been a political football used by both the left and the right. Are these simply highly publicized but isolated incidents, or do they represent a broader trend of partisanship shaping how people make economic decisions even in the absence of a public campaign calling for a specific boycott?

We conducted four experiments to address these questions by exploring the role of partisanship in shaping economic behavior. (The details of our analysis will be available in our forthcoming article in the *American Journal of Political Science*.) In the first experiment, a field study carried out in an online labor market, we assessed whether individuals are more likely to demand higher wages when they learn that their boss's political party is different from their own. The second study examined whether people are less likely to purchase a heavily discounted gift card if the seller was affiliated with the other party, but more likely to do so if the seller is from their own party; the third study replicated this in a larger online marketplace. In our fourth study, an incentivized survey, we offered participants the ability to make money, but we told them that we would also make a donation to the opposing political party. Each of these experiments allowed us to assess how participants' economic choices and actions are shaped by their partisan commitments.

All four experiments offer evidence that partisanship influences economic behavior, even when it is costly. For example, in the labor market experiment people were willing to work for less money for fellow partisans; this effect is as large as the effect of factors like relevant employment experience. When presented with a purchasing opportunity, consumers were almost twice as likely to engage in a transaction when their partisanship matched the seller's. In our survey experiment, three-quarters of the subjects refused a higher monetary payment to avoid helping the other party—in other words, they preferred to make themselves worse off so that they would not benefit the other party. Taken together, these results clearly indicate that the trends we highlighted earlier are unlikely to be isolated incidents. The impact of party attachments on economic choices is likely to be stronger and more widespread than generally recognized.

Our results highlight another point about partisanship in contemporary society: It has become an important social identity. It extends beyond particular policy beliefs or support for specific politicians. Our findings show that people evaluate the exact same transaction differently based on whether the other party is a Democrat or a Republican, even though their partisanship ostensibly provides no information about their quality as an employer or seller. (Other studies have found that partisanship shapes how people judge the seriousness of criminal acts, the suitability of someone for a merit scholarship, or whether they would want to date someone.) The mechanism behind this difference remains murky. People may infer characteristics such as trustworthiness based on partisanship, or may simply be reacting emotionally. Either explanation would fit the patterns we have found in our work. But what seems clear is that partisanship's power is not limited to politics.

Our results call for paying greater attention to potential discrimination based on partisan affiliation. To date, few social norms constrain such behavior, and because social media makes political expression increasingly visible, it is now common to know the partisan attachments of those around us. Our analysis suggests that partisan-based discrimination may occur even in the most ordinary economic settings, and not just in response to highly publicized campaigns. As such, this type of discrimination should be the subject of more systematic scrutiny—not only from scholars but also from businesspeople, workers, and consumers. Lastly, our study raises the possibility that corporate executives who inject politics into their businesses can boost support among those who agree with them, but may alienate those who do not.

Periodical and Internet Sources Bibliography

The following articles have been selected to supplement the diverse views presented in this chapter.

Alan Abramowitz and Jennifer McCoy, "United States: Racial Resentment, Negative Partisanship, and Polarization in Trump's America," *Annals of the American Academy*, January 2019. https://journals.sagepub.com/doi/pdf/10.1177/0002716218811309.

John Avlon, "The Civil War's Surprising, and Alarmingly Familiar, Origins," *Vanity Fair*, February 10, 2022. https://www.vanityfair.com/news/2022/02/the-civil-wars-surprising-and-alarmingly-familiar-origins.

Ronald Brownstein, "America Is Growing Apart, Possibly for Good," *Atlantic*, June 24, 2022. https://www.theatlantic.com/politics/archive/2022/06/red-and-blue-state-divide-is-growing-michael-podhorzer-newsletter/661377/.

Drew Desilver, "The Polarization in Today's Congress Has Roots that Go Back Decades," Pew Research Center, March 10, 2022. https://www.pewresearch.org/fact-tank/2022/03/10/the-polarization-in-todays-congress-has-roots-that-go-back-decades/.

Blake Hounshell, "Measuring America's Divide: 'It's Gotten Worse,'" *New York Times*, July 27, 2022. https://www.nytimes.com/2022/07/27/us/politics/vanderbilt-unity-index.html.

Rachel Kleinfeld, "The Rise in Political Violence in the United States and the Damage to Democracy," Carnegie Endowment for International Peace, March 31, 2022. https://carnegieendowment.org/2022/03/31/rise-in-political-violence-in-united-states-and-damage-to-our-democracy-pub-87584.

Chris McGreal, "US Political Violence Is Surging, but Talk of a Civil War Is Exaggerated—Isn't It?" *Guardian*, August 20, 2022. https://www.theguardian.com/us-news/2022/aug/20/us-political-violence-civil-war.

Rani Molla, "Social Media Is Making a Bad Political Situation Worse," *Vox*, November 10, 2020. https://www.vox.com/recode/21534345/polarization-election-social-media-filter-bubble.

Peter Suciu, "Does Social Media Make the Political Divide Worse?" *Forbes*, October 30, 2019. https://www.forbes.com/sites/petersuciu/2019/10/30/does-social-media-make-the-political-divide-worse/?sh=42a430fa6e3a.

Jeremi Suri, "Our Nation Is Still Divided Along the Battle Lines of the Civil War," *TIME*, May 6, 2022. https://time.com/6174297/america-divided-civil-war/.

CHAPTER 3

Is America's Great Divide Unique?

Chapter Preface

The United States is far from the only country that has become increasingly polarized in recent years. In the United Kingdom, the "Brexit" referendum in 2016 and ultimate withdrawal from the European Union in 2020 served as a major source of tension among the British public. In other European countries, political parties with more extreme political views—such as nationalist, far right, and even neo-Nazi parties—have gained traction. This has occurred in countries such as France, Italy, Sweden, Hungary, and Poland.[1] This trend is not unique to Europe and the U.S., either. Other countries around the world that are facing this issue include Bangladesh, Brazil, Colombia, India, Indonesia, Kenya, Malaysia, and Sri Lanka.[2] In general, democracies around the world have been facing increasing levels of polarization in recent years.

However, as some of the viewpoints in this chapter argue, there are certain characteristics of polarization in the U.S. that distinguish it from the divisions in other countries, and that may in fact make it worse. In a 2020 paper published by the National Bureau of Economic Research, there has been a greater increase in affective polarization—or the way voters from one political party feel about those from the other party—in the U.S. than in any of the other eight countries surveyed.[3] The researchers speculate that this is caused in part by the nature of party politics in the U.S., which has increasingly been characterized by an alignment of political identity with race, ideology, and religious belief.[4] The authors of other viewpoints in this chapter agree with the assertion that division in the U.S. has strong sociological roots.

But despite how divided the U.S. may seem, some experts argue that although American politics are highly polarized, the American public is not nearly as divided. As Ken Stern asserts, "every day, America is being misled by the political parties, our political leaders, and the press."[5] It benefits politicians and the press to make American voters feel a strong emotional reaction to political issues and the opposing party to strengthen the party's political base and increase engagement with the media. However, on many key issues, Americans from both political parties are not nearly as divided as they seem, according to some experts.

The viewpoints in this chapter take a closer look at polarization not just in America, but around the world, and consider how division in the U.S. stacks up. The viewpoints also examine what causes polarization in America and whether it actually is as big of an issue as it seems.

Notes

1. Zachary B. Wolf, "How the Far Right Is Surging in Europe," CNN, September 26, 2022. https://www.cnn.com/2022/09/26/politics/europe-far-right-what-matters/index.html.
2. Thomas Carothers and Andrew O'Donohue, "How to Understand the Global Spread of Political Polarization," Carnegie Endowment for International Peace, October 1, 2019. https://carnegieendowment.org/2019/10/01/how-to-understand-global-spread-of-political-polarization-pub-79893.
3. Jill Kimball, "U.S. Is Polarizing Faster Than Other Democracies, Study Finds," Brown University, January 21, 2020. https://www.brown.edu/news/2020-01-21/polarization.
4. *Ibid.*
5. Ken Stern, "Americans Aren't as Divided as You Think," *POLITICO*, November 19, 2017. https://www.politico.com/magazine/story/2017/11/19/americans-divided-politics-unity-liberal-bubble-215843/.

VIEWPOINT 1

> *"In the U.S., affective polarization has increased more dramatically since the late 1970s than in the eight other countries they examined."*

America Is Polarizing Faster than Other Countries

Jill Kimball

This viewpoint examines a study conducted in 2020 on affective polarization in multiple countries. Although the United States is not the only country to experience rising levels of polarization, it is the country where this increase has been most pronounced. One of the reasons for dramatic increases in polarization in the U.S. is the increased alignment of political identity with ideological and social identity, which has caused the parties to become increasingly homogenized. The rise of 24-hour partisan news in the U.S. is also identified as a cause. These factors make the U.S. uniquely at risk of polarization. Jill Kimball is a communications manager and writer covering the humanities and social sciences at Brown University.

As you read, consider the following questions:

1. What are the other countries examined in the study referenced in this viewpoint?

"U.S. Is Polarizing Faster Than Other Democracies, Study Finds," by Jill Kimball, Brown University, January 21, 2020. Reprinted by permission.

2. What other countries experienced an increase in polarization over the previous 40 years?
3. According to the author, does the data suggest that increased internet use plays a major role in polarization?

Political polarization among Americans has grown rapidly in the last 40 years—more than in Canada, the United Kingdom, Australia or Germany—a phenomenon possibly due to increased racial division, the rise of partisan cable news, and changes in the composition of the Democratic and Republican parties.

That's according to new research co-authored by Jesse Shapiro, a professor of political economy at Brown University. The study, conducted alongside Stanford University economists Levi Boxell and Matthew Gentzkow, was released on Monday, Jan. 20, as a National Bureau of Economic Research working paper.

In the study, Shapiro and colleagues present the first ever multi-nation evidence on long-term trends in "affective polarization"—a phenomenon in which citizens feel more negatively toward other political parties than toward their own. They found that in the U.S., affective polarization has increased more dramatically since the late 1970s than in the eight other countries they examined—the U.K., Canada, Australia, New Zealand, Germany, Switzerland, Norway, and Sweden.

"A lot of analysis on polarization is focused on the U.S., so we thought it could be interesting to put the U.S. in context and see whether it is part of a global trend or whether it looks more exceptional," Shapiro said. "We found that the trend in the U.S. is indeed exceptional."

Using data from four decades of public opinion surveys conducted in the nine countries, the researchers used a so-called "feeling thermometer" to rate attitudes on a scale from 0 to 100, where 0 reflected no negative feelings toward other parties. They found that in 1978, the average American rated the members of their own political party 27 points higher than members of the other major party. By 2016, Americans were rating their own party 45.9 points higher than the other party, on average. In other words, negative feelings toward members of the other party compared to one's own party increased by an average of 4.8 points per decade.

The researchers found that polarization had also risen in Canada, New Zealand, and Switzerland in the last 40 years, but to a lesser extent. In the UK, Australia, Germany, Norway, and Sweden, polarization decreased.

Why has the U.S. become so much more polarized? Shapiro said it may be partly because, since the 1970s, major political parties have become increasingly aligned with certain ideologies, races, and religious identities. For example, Republicans are now more likely to be religious, while Democrats are more likely to be secular.

"There's evidence that within the U.S., the two major political parties have become more homogeneous in certain ways, including ideologically and socially," Shapiro said. "So when you identify with a certain party and you're looking across the aisle, the people you're looking at are more different from you than they were a few decades ago."

That "party sorting" seems to be less pronounced in some of the other countries included in the study, Shapiro said—but it has perhaps played a role in deepening divisions in Canada.

Another explanation for the increase in polarization—one that also seems relatively unique to the U.S., according to Shapiro—is the rise of 24-hour partisan cable news. Shapiro noted that in the countries where political polarization has fallen in the last four decades, public broadcasting received more public funding than it did in the U.S.

The trio argue that the data speak against the rise of the internet as a major cause of political polarization because all nine countries have seen a pronounced rise in internet use, but not all of them have seen a rise in polarization. The conclusion is consistent with other studies they have conducted, including one in 2018 that cast doubt on the hypothesized role of the web in the 2016 U.S. presidential election and another in 2017 that concluded greater internet use among Americans is not associated with faster growth in polarization.

Shapiro said that understanding the root causes of political polarization, both in the U.S. and elsewhere in the world, could help politicians and citizens alike understand how the phenomenon may be driving their decisions and preferences—and it could ultimately reveal strategies for bridging divides.

"There are good reasons to think that when people in different political camps cease to respect each other, it's harder to make political compromises and create good public policy," Shapiro said. "There's also some evidence that a person's political identity can influence their behavior—what they buy, where they live, who they hire. If we can understand what's driving partisan divides, we may be able to take steps to reduce them."

From these, we extracted cross-cutting findings. And the sheer diversity of our cases—in terms of societal makeup, political institutions, and economic development—opened our eyes to discoveries that we might have missed if we had looked only at the United States and Europe.

Q: Did you see a similar pattern in polarized democracies around the world?

A: The degree of similarity we found across countries was startling. Even in democracies as different as Colombia, Kenya, and Poland, many of the roots, patterns, and drivers of polarization were the same.

Particularly striking was just how decisive polarizing leaders often are. Figures like Narendra Modi in India, Jarosław Kaczyński in Poland, and Recep Tayyip Erdoğan in Turkey have relentlessly inflamed basic divisions and entrenched them throughout society (often with resounding electoral success). They've aggravated tensions not only by demonizing opponents and curtailing democratic processes but also by pushing for radical changes—like a total ban on abortion in Poland.

Amplifying the effect of these divisive figures is the technologically fueled disruption of the media industry, especially the rise of social media. Opposition leaders often fan the flames as well by responding with antidemocratic and confrontational tactics of their own. In Turkey, for instance, the head of the main opposition party stoked tensions by calling on the military to oppose Erdoğan's potential bid for the presidency in 2007.

Many other drivers of polarization struck us as surprising, even counterintuitive. You might expect, for instance, that a growing economy would ease polarization. Yet we found that in some places, such as India, it actually made things worse. Indeed, the growth of India's middle class has led to rising support for polarizing Hindu nationalist narratives.

We also found that patronage and corruption—two decidedly antidemocratic practices—can temporarily reduce polarization by helping politicians build very big tents. In the long term, however, the political rot that this causes frequently leaves voters disgusted with the traditional parties and fuels the rise of divisive populist figures, like Hugo Chávez in Venezuela and Jair Bolsonaro in Brazil.

Q: What happens to democracies when polarization intensifies?

A: Severe polarization damages all institutions essential to democracy.

It routinely undermines the independence of the judiciary, as politicians attack the courts as biased or pack them with loyalists. It reduces legislatures either to gridlock or to a rubberstamp function. In presidential systems, it frequently leads to the abuse of executive powers and promotes the toxic view that the president represents only their supporters, rather than the country as a whole.

Perhaps most fundamentally, polarization shatters informal but crucial norms of tolerance and moderation—like conceding peacefully after an electoral defeat—that keep political competition within bounds.

These consequences generate a vicious cycle of rising polarization. Attacks on the judiciary, for example, only diminish its capacity to arbitrate conflict and heighten distrust between the opposing sides.

Polarization also reverberates throughout the society as whole, poisoning everyday interactions and relationships. Turkey is a particularly jarring example: almost eight out of ten people there would not want their daughter to marry someone who votes for the party they most dislike. Nearly three-quarters would not even want to do business with such a person.

Partisan conflict takes a heavy toll on civil society as well, often leading to the demonization of activists and human rights defenders. More seriously still, divisions can contribute to a spike in hate crimes and political violence: India, Poland, and the United States have all seen such increases in recent years.

Q: What about polarization in the United States? Is it similar to polarization in other countries?

A: The more we looked at the experiences of other divided democracies, the more we realized that U.S. polarization stands out as unusual. It has several distinctive features, and unfortunately, all of them spell trouble for U.S. democracy.

In the first place, polarization in the United States isn't primarily the result of polarizing politicians stoking divisions, as in most other countries. It has deep societal roots and is the outcome of a profound sociocultural struggle between contending conservative and progressive visions of the country. Consequently, U.S. polarization is not something that political leaders can easily reverse, even if they want to.

Intense partisanship has gripped the United States for an unusually long time and thus become ingrained in social and political life. Today's divisions date back at least to the 1960s and have been steadily intensifying for over 50 years. Most other current cases of polarization are more recent in origin.

A final distinctive and perhaps even unique feature of U.S. polarization is the powerful alignment of ethnicity, ideology, and religion on each side of the divide—what we call the "iron triangle" of U.S. polarization. In most other countries, just one or two of those three identity divisions is at the root of polarization; in the United States, all three are. As a result, America's polarization is unusually encompassing and sharp.

While partisan warfare hasn't eroded democracy in the United States to the same extent that it has in, say, Bangladesh or Turkey, it is testing our democratic guardrails in serious ways.

Q: What can be done to defeat polarization and bring a country together?

A: Once a society becomes deeply divided, it is very difficult to heal. Before talking about remedial actions, it's crucial to understand why this problem is so thorny and difficult to overcome.

Polarization tends to escalate at a dizzyingly fast pace, often in the span of just a few years. Just look at how rapidly the 2016 Brexit referendum has ripped the United Kingdom apart.

Polarization then entrenches itself and becomes self-perpetuating. Polarizing actions and reactions feed on each other, dragging countries into a downward spiral of anger and division.

And while the consequences of polarization are punishing, they don't necessarily galvanize a government to respond, because the politicians who play the most significant role in exacerbating polarization mostly benefit from it and bear little of the cost.

Yet despite these challenges, our research shows that a wide range of actors have tried inventive ways of addressing the problem—and sometimes achieved encouraging results.

Q: What are some ways to counter polarization?

A: Our work identifies and analyzes eight different types of remedial actions, ranging from dialogue efforts and media reforms to international action. We'll highlight just three examples here.

For one, several promising efforts to limit polarization have focused on institutional reforms, such as decentralizing political power or changing electoral rules. Kenya, for instance, adopted a new constitution in 2010 that sought to ease ferocious competition for national office by giving regional officials greater autonomy and control over state resources. But important reforms don't always require changing a country's constitution: in the United States, for example, Maine passed legislation in 2016 to enact ranked-choice voting, a system that favors centrist candidates and discourages negative campaigning.

Other efforts have involved legal or judicial action to limit polarization and majoritarianism—the idea that the feelings and rights of the minority should not constrain leaders with majority support. In India, for example, the Supreme Court has spoken out in defense of democratic institutions and demanded greater accountability for hate crimes and political violence.

Political leadership can also play a crucial role in de-escalating partisan divides. In Ecuador, President Lenín Moreno has rejected the polarizing tactics of his predecessor, even though the two come from the same political party. And in Turkey, opposition parties have achieved modest success by uniting to form a coalition: their candidate for mayor of Istanbul won a resounding victory in 2019 with a campaign that emphasized overcoming divisions.

Still, these initiatives are small compared to the larger forces driving polarization. Democracies will need to rise to this challenge in new and determined ways if they are to swim successfully against the swelling global current of polarization.

Q: When you were researching the book, did you find out anything you didn't expect?

A: When we looked at the fierce polarization in many countries, we expected to find deep-seated differences between the opposing sides. So we were taken aback to discover that sometimes those differences seem slight.

Take the example of Bangladesh: acrimonious political competition there has led to violence, election fraud, and a complete breakdown of democracy. But polarization isn't rooted in any fundamental ethnic, ideological, or religious division among voters. It is almost entirely the result of power struggles within a political elite that plays up and manufactures divisions.

That finding gave us pause: it showed us that the potential for destructive divisions exists in almost all societies, even ones that seem relatively homogeneous. Our research underscores just how vulnerable democracies are to polarization—and how powerful the factors fueling divisions are.

VIEWPOINT 3

> "On several big issues, the center of gravity among conservatives in the U.S. stands further to the right than it does among their ideological counterparts in Europe. Liberals in the U.S. have moved further to the left in the past four years."

Certain Political Topics Are Far More Controversial in America than in Other Countries

David Lauter

In this viewpoint, David Lauter discusses the findings of a Pew Research Center survey examining how political divisions in the U.S. compare to those in major Western European democracies. Though many draw comparisons between the contentious Brexit debate in the UK and discussions of immigration in the U.S., Lauter argues that the data suggests there are some key differences. Restrictionist views of national identity are much more common among American conservatives compared to conservatives in other countries, according to the data, meaning more conservative Americans believe that certain characteristics are necessary to truly belong as an American. David Lauter is a senior editor at the Los Angeles Times.

"Essential Politics: The Left-Right Split Is Far Bigger in the U.S. Than in Europe—and It's Growing," Los Angeles Times, May 7, 2021. © 2021 David Lauter. Used with permission.

America's Great Divide

As you read, consider the following questions:

1. What were the four countries included in the survey referenced in this viewpoint?
2. Did a decrease in restrictive views on national identity occur across the political spectrum in all four countries surveyed?
3. What percent of U.S. Christians identify as being on the right politically? How does this compare to the percentage in Germany?

Anyone who has watched U.S. politics in recent years knows that a widening gap between left and right, Democrat and Republican, has defined our era. Hardly a week passes without fresh evidence.

Americans—and some Europeans—have often talked of similar divisions in Western Europe's major democracies. Divisive issues like Brexit in the U.K. and the rights of religious minorities in France drive comparisons to U.S. polarization.

But the U.S. differs notably from those other countries: Our ideological gaps are much wider on big cultural issues, according to a major new study by the Pew Research Center.

Pew began to study the comparison during Britain's divisive debate over leaving the European Union and the campaign leading up to Donald Trump's election as president. Researchers "really wanted to see what the concepts of nationalism and cosmopolitanism mean in the modern era," said Pew's Laura Silver, one of the lead authors.

What they found provides insights into America's divides and how those differ from other wealthy democracies. The numbers, based on surveys of more than 4,000 adults in the U.S., France, Germany and the U.K., provide important context for understanding the Republican Party's continuing evolution away from the country's business establishment and toward becoming a more populist party of the right.

Questions of National Identity

On several big issues, the center of gravity among conservatives in the U.S. stands further to the right than it does among their ideological counterparts in Europe, Pew's numbers show. On the other end of the spectrum, liberals in the U.S. have moved further to the left in the past four years.

A large share of U.S. conservatives support restrictionist views of national identity, such as believing that "truly belonging" requires being native born or being a Christian. A large number also believe that discrimination against minority groups is an exaggerated problem.

Since 2016, across all four countries surveyed, the public has shifted toward less restrictive stands on issues of national identity. In Europe, that shift took place across the ideological spectrum. In the U.S., it did not.

U.S. liberals moved left—in some cases further left than their European counterparts. U.S. conservatives, however, started off further to the right than Europeans and did not move.

"Generally, we saw gaps closing in Europe," said Silver. "The gap didn't close comparably in the U.S."

In 2016, for example, majorities in both the U.S. and the U.K., and about half of those surveyed in France, said that to be "truly" a member of their societies, it was at least somewhat important to be native born. About a third of Germans held the same view.

Now, the share holding that view has dropped a lot in all four countries—to about 1 in 3 in the U.S., U.K. and France and 1 in 4 in Germany. Each of the national surveys has a margin of error of about four percentage points.

In the three European countries, the drop did not vary much by ideology. In the U.S., liberals shifted much more than conservatives, so the U.S. divide widened.

Pew also asked if being Christian was an important part of being "truly American" or British, French or German. The share saying yes declined in all four countries. So has the share saying that to truly belong, a person must observe the country's customs and traditions.

As with the question about native birth, however, in the U.S., the overall decline has been accompanied by a widening ideological gap. On the question of following national customs, the share of self-identified liberals and moderates calling it an important part if being truly American declined about 20 points. The share of conservatives did not budge.

Responses on a fourth topic—language—underscored the unique nature of the U.S. divide.

In the three European countries, close to 9 in 10 people across the board say being able to speak the dominant language is at least somewhat important to belonging. That's also true of about 9 in 10 American conservatives.

But among American liberals, that view has declined sharply over the past four years: Just over half now say that speaking English is at least somewhat important for belonging in the U.S.

On that question it's American liberals who stand out as different from their European counterparts; on others, U.S. conservatives stand out.

About a third of U.S. conservatives, for example, say that being native born is an important part of belonging; in the three European countries, no more than 1 in 4 say that.

Asked which is the bigger problem, people not recognizing discrimination where it does exist or people seeing discrimination where it does not exist, majorities in Britain, Germany and the U.S. said failure to recognize discrimination is the bigger problem. In France, the public closely splits on that issue.

In all four countries, a gap separates left and right on that question, with conservatives more likely to say the bigger problem is claiming discrimination where it doesn't exist. In the U.S., however, the ideological gap is twice as large as in the U.K. or France and four times larger than in Germany.

Similarly, the ideological split in the U.S. is about twice as large as in any of the three European countries when people are asked if their country would be better off if it "sticks to its traditions and way of life" versus being "open to changes regarding its traditions and way of life."

Religion is one of the factors that contributes to the larger ideological gap in the U.S. America remains more religious than most European societies, and white Christians, in particular, have become a mainstay for Republicans.

"Christians stand out on many issues from non-Christians," Silver noted. "They are more likely to say there is a great deal of discrimination against Christians in their society and to say that being Christian is essential to truly being part of their country's citizenry than non-Christians. They are also more likely to say other key factors—including speaking the language and being born in the country—are essential components of national belonging."

Not only are Christians a larger share of the population in the U.S., American Christians are more likely than European ones to identify as being on the right politically, Silver said; 52 percent of U.S. Christians did so, compared with 48 percent in France, 36 percent in the U.K. and 27 percent in Germany.

The positions taken by a large share of U.S. conservatives put them in line with European supporters of right-wing, populist parties such as the National Front in France and the nationalist Alternative for Germany, the survey found.

That, in turn, helps explain the continuing strength of the populist faction of the GOP. Trump benefited from the rise of populism in the party, but as the Pew survey helps make clear, he didn't invent it, and it's not likely to dissipate whenever he departs from the political scene.

VIEWPOINT 4

> "There are many reasons for our increasing polarization, but one reason is that the big bully pulpits in America are now in the hands of people who benefit from anger and conflict."

America Is Not as Divided as It Seems

Ken Stern

In this viewpoint, which was published in late 2017, Ken Stern argues that America is not nearly as divided as we are led to believe by politicians and the press. However, disagreement between Americans doesn't have to lead to hate, and in fact Americans across the political spectrum do not disagree with each other as much as they believe. It benefits politicians to create a strong emotional reaction on political issues to gain support, and benefits the media to present exaggerated stories of division to get a larger audience. However, it does not benefit the American public or democracy. Ken Stern is president of Palisades Media Ventures and former CEO of NPR.

As you read, consider the following questions:

1. How does the author identify politically?
2. According to the Gallup poll referenced in this viewpoint, has the percentage of Americans who think abortion

"Americans Aren't as Divided as You Think," by Ken Stern, November 19, 2017. Reprinted by permission of POLITICO LLC. Copyright 2016 POLITICO LLC.

| 122

should be legal in at least some circumstances changed considerably over the previous 40 years?
3. Who does Stern hold accountable for the increase in polarization?

Every day, America is being misled by the political parties, our political leaders, and the press. We are told that the other side—whether it's liberals or conservatives, Democrats or Republicans—are not just wrong on the issues, but full of destructive intent. The other side is full of deplorables or white nationalists or snowflakes or, worse yet, globalists. We are assured that the other side despises American values and is intent on destroying the country as we know it. We believe all these things.

Here's something to talk about at your Thanksgiving dinner table: None of this is true. I'm a life-long Democrat and have a resume that practically bleeds blue: a couple turns in Democratic politics, almost a decade running NPR, and degrees from Yale Law School and Haverford College. But last year, spurred by a fear that Red and Blue America were drifting irrevocably apart, I decided to venture out from my overwhelmingly Democratic neighborhood and safely Democratic life, and engage Republicans where they live, work and pray. I found an America far different from the one depicted in the press and imagined for us by politicians.

I sat in the pews of tiny evangelical churches in Virginia and mega-churches in Houston and was moved by the passion of many of my fellow congregants to help the poor and those who live in the shadows. It wasn't just empty Sunday words, but weekday deeds by many of my new co-religionists to support refugees, feed the hungry, and house the homeless. I traveled into some of the most economically depressed areas of our country and met coal miners without coal mines and mill workers without mills. It didn't seem so deplorable that many of them were angry that the economies of their communities and the health of their families were in a three-decade freefall, and were eager to protest a government and a political and media establishment that were willing to accept their pain as a necessary byproduct of free trade or the fight against global warming. Over the course of a year, I traveled from churches to conservative think tanks to NASCAR races and even to Tea Party meetings, and I was almost always able to find more points of agreement and commonality than I thought possible.

Don't get me wrong. I met a few less attractive types along the way—people who would openly assure me of the vast global conspiracies that control the White House—and I spent enough time on the Breitbart comment pages to have my faith in humanity weakened a time or two. But these instances were far outnumbered

THE U.S. IS NOWHERE NEAR AS POLARIZED AS IT WAS DURING THE CIVIL WAR

It has become common to say that the United States in 2020 is more divided politically and culturally than at any other point in our national past.

As a historian who has written and taught about the Civil War era for several decades, I know that current divisions pale in comparison to those of the mid-19th century.

Between Abraham Lincoln's election in November 1860 and the surrender of Robert E. Lee's Confederate army at Appomattox in April 1865, the nation literally broke apart.

More than 3 million men took up arms, and hundreds of thousands of black and white civilians in the Confederacy became refugees. Four million enslaved African Americans were freed from bondage.

After the war ended, the country soon entered a decade of virulent, and often violent, disagreement about how best to order a biracial society in the absence of slavery.

To compare anything that has transpired in the past few years to this cataclysmic upheaval represents a spectacular lack of understanding about American history.

by the many points of commonality I found along the way. As Sam Adams, an openly gay mayor who worked closely with Portland's evangelical community, told me, we've all fallen into a trap: "If we disagree, we must hate each other. If the media portrays us, certain aspects of us or certain individuals hating each other, then that must be true for everybody … There are things we don't agree on as a liberal Democrat and as an evangelical leader … We can agree to disagree on gay marriage and disagree on abortion but we probably agree on eight of 10 things that are important to society."

We loathe the other side far more than we used to—polls show that most Americans now believe the other political party threatens the nation's well-being, and a stunning number of us

Internal Fractures, Furious War

Americans were thus forced to face the reality that the political system established by the founding generation had failed to manage internal fractures and positioned the United States and the newly established Confederacy to engage in open warfare.

The scale and fury of the ensuing combat underscores the utter inappropriateness of claims that the United States is more divided now than ever before.

Four years of civil war produced at least 620,000 military deaths—the equivalent of approximately 6.5 million dead in the United States of 2020.

The institution of slavery—and especially its potential spread from the South and border states into federal territories—was the key to this slaughter because it provoked the series of crises that eventually proved intractable.

No political issue in 2020 approaches slavery in the mid-19th century in terms of potential divisiveness.

"Think the US Is More Polarized Than Ever? You Don't Know History", by Gary W. Gallagher, The Conversation, February 14, 2020. https://theconversation.com/think-the-us-is-more-polarized-than-ever-you-dont-know-history-131600. Licensed under CC BY 4.0 International.

now disapprove of our children engaging in mixed marriages—not racially mixed, not religiously mixed, but politically mixed. But the odd thing is that while we are far more politically polarized, we are not more issue polarized than in the past. It is counterintuitive in this age of anger, but on the issues, we still tend to be a fairly agreeable and moderate people. As Morris Fiorina, the Stanford political scientist, has observed, "on most issues, attitudes continue to cluster in the middle rather than lump up on the extremes."

You can see this more closely when you peer into data on a specific matter like abortion, one of the most divisive issues of our day. Gallup has been following abortion opinion closely for more than 40 years, and what is most extraordinary when you look at the numbers is how opinions are both constant and moderate. By far, the largest group of Americans has always been those who think abortion should be legal under some circumstances. That number has never left the incredibly tight range of 48 to 55 percent. And when you start asking Americans about specific abortion-related fact patterns, as Fiorina and his fellow researcher Jon Krosnick once did, even the views of those who described themselves as "always pro-life" or "always pro-choice" begin to converge. The "always pro-life" group weakened considerably when the woman's life was said to be at stake and the "always pro-choice" crowd thinned significantly when the abortion was because the mother disliked the gender of the child. Even on this supposedly most controversial and polarizing issue, the American impulse is towards moderation and consensus.

You wouldn't know any of this by listening to the political parties or by looking at their platforms in 2016. The Republican Party trumpeted the most "pro-life, pro-family" platform ever, while the Democrats bragged that its platform went "further than previous Democratic platforms on women's reproductive rights." It is disconcerting to see the parties brag about their moves toward the extremes when their voters remain solidly and resolutely in the middle. This is all because the parties are solidly in the hands of activists more interested in furthering their own agendas than reflecting the views of the broader public.

There are many reasons for our increasing polarization, but one reason is that the big bully pulpits in America are now in the hands of people who benefit from anger and conflict. It's not just the internet trolls and red-faced media, but the political parties and their candidates. The Democratic Party has largely eschewed policy reform in favor of #resistance to President Trump. As for the Republicans, exposing and exploiting division is their most identifiable strategy. Compromise and nuance are lost in this inflammatory age. All of this may make good copy but it's terrible for democracy and we won't restore our sense of one country, one nation, one civil society until we stop seeing the other side as "the other side" and start seeing them again as our friends, neighbors, and countrymen. That takes a bit of a journey from where we are now, but perhaps it a journey in the spirit of the holidays. As Atticus Finch, a hero of a different age, once said, "You never really understand a person until you consider things from his point of view."

America's Great Divide

Periodical and Internet Sources Bibliography

The following articles have been selected to supplement the diverse views presented in this chapter.

Fernando Casal Bértoa and José Rama, "Polarization: What Do We Know and What Can We Do About It?" *Frontiers in Political Science*, June 30, 2021. https://www.frontiersin.org/articles/10.3389/fpos.2021.687695/full.

Morris P. Fiorina, "Polarization Is Not the Problem," *Stanford Magazine*, May 2018. https://stanfordmag.org/contents/polarization-is-not-the-problem.

David Lauter, "Researchers Asked People Worldwide About Divisiveness. Guess Where U.S. Ranked," *Los Angeles Times*, October 15, 2021. https://www.latimes.com/politics/newsletter/2021-10-15/us-most-divided-nation-in-worldwide-survey-essential-politics.

Trymaine Lee, "A Vast Wealth Gap, Driven by Segregation, Redlining, Evictions and Exclusion, Separates Black and White America," *New York Times*, August 14, 2019. https://www.nytimes.com/interactive/2019/08/14/magazine/racial-wealth-gap.html.

Jennifer McCoy and Benjamin Press, "What Happens When Democracies Become Perniciously Polarized?" Carnegie Endowment for International Peace, January 18, 2022. https://carnegieendowment.org/2022/01/18/what-happens-when-democracies-become-perniciously-polarized-pub-86190.

Joe Myers, "These Charts Show the Growing Inequality Between the World's Richest and Poorest," World Economic Forum, December 10, 2021. https://www.weforum.org/agenda/2021/12/global-income-inequality-gap-report-rich-poor/.

Anshu Siripurapu, "The U.S. Inequality Debate," Council on Foreign Relations, April 20, 2022. https://www.cfr.org/backgrounder/us-inequality-debate.

Matthew Stewart, "The 9.9 Percent Is the New American Aristocracy," *Atlantic*, June 2018. https://www.theatlantic.com/magazine/archive/2018/06/the-birth-of-a-new-american-aristocracy/559130/.

Grant Suneson and Samuel Stebbins, "The 15 Countries Have the Widest Gaps Between Rich and Poor," *USA Today*, May 28, 2019. https://www.usatoday.com/story/money/2019/05/28/countries-with-the-widest-gaps-between-rich-and-poor/39510157/.

Robert B. Talisse, "Not All Polarization Is Bad, but the US Could Be in Trouble," *Conversation*, January 3, 2022. https://theconversation.com/not-all-polarization-is-bad-but-the-us-could-be-in-trouble-173833.

CHAPTER 4

Can America Become Less Divided?

Chapter Preface

According to numerous experts, one of the major issues associated with increasing division in America is a loss of trust. This loss of trust is towards the government, the media, other institutions, and fellow Americans—particularly those of the opposite political party. A 2018 survey from the Pew Research Center found that 75 percent of Americans do not believe the federal government is worthy of higher levels of trust at this point.[1] However, the research suggests that although there is a crisis of trust among the American public, finding ways to rebuild trust is a major priority for most Americans. The same Pew survey found that 68 percent of Americans believe that it is very important for trust in the federal government to be restored and 58 percent consider it very important to build faith in fellow Americans.[2]

Another issue the experts in this chapter consider is the role psychology plays in division and what can be done to change the way Americans react to those of different social and political groups on a psychological level. As viewpoints in previous chapters have discussed, one of the reasons that polarization in the U.S. is so strong and so unique is because it is affective in nature, or related to emotion. Research from the organization Beyond Conflict suggests that Americans tend to assume that members of the opposite political party have much more negative opinions of them than they actually do. In fact, the organization found that "Americans incorrectly believe that members of the other party dehumanize, dislike, and disagree with them about twice as much as they actually do."[3] This misperception plays a role in promoting greater division, so correcting this misunderstanding can help to address this issue.

Finally, some experts suggest that changing the structure of American politics could go a long way in cutting down on division. The two-party system creates a political environment in which the two main parties are pitted against one another. By allowing more political parties to be actively involved in the political process and encouraging more competition among candidates, polarization could decrease and faith in the government could increase. However, some experts argue that because the two-party system is so deeply engrained in American politics, it could be nearly impossible to change this.

The viewpoints in this chapter consider the major issues causing division in America today. At the same time, they examine ways in which these issues could be addressed to lead to a less polarized, more cooperative future.

Notes

1. Lee Rainie, Scott Keeter, and Andrew Perrin, "Trust and Distrust in America," Pew Research Center, July 22, 2019. https://www.pewresearch.org/politics/2019/07/22/trust-and-distrust-in-america/.
2. *Ibid.*
3. "Understanding the Psychology That Drives Us Apart," Beyond Conflict. https://beyondconflictint.org/americas-divided-mind/.

VIEWPOINT 1

> "Many people no longer think the federal government can actually be a force for good or change in their lives. This kind of apathy and disengagement will lead to an even worse and less representative government."

Distrust in the Government and Other Americans Makes Reconciliation Challenging

Lee Rainie, Scott Keeter, and Andrew Perrin

In the following excerpted viewpoint, Lee Rainie, Scott Keeter, and Andrew Perrin examine the results of a 2018 survey conducted by the Pew Research Center. The survey covered multiple trust-related issues, including how much adults trust the government, how much they trust their fellow Americans, and whether they think these levels of trust need to be improved. Most Americans agree that trust in the government and others has declined in recent years, and they also agree that it needs to be improved. Lee Rainie is director of internet and technology research at Pew Research Center, Scott Keeter is the center's senior survey advisor, and Andrew Perrin is a former research analyst.

"Trust and Distrust in America," by Lee Rainie, Scott Keeter, and Andrew Perrin, Pew Research Center, July 22, 2019. Reprinted by permission.

As you read, consider the following questions:

1. What percent of Americans polled in this viewpoint consider it very important to repair the public's confidence in the federal government?
2. How does the percentage of young adults with a low amount of personal trust for other people compare to the percentage of older adults who feel this way?
3. What are some of the differences in how Democrats and Republicans view the issue of trust listed in this viewpoint?

Trust is an essential elixir for public life and neighborly relations, and when Americans think about trust these days, they worry. Two-thirds of adults think other Americans have little or no confidence in the federal government. Majorities believe the public's confidence in the U.S. government and in each other is shrinking, and most believe a shortage of trust in government and in other citizens makes it harder to solve some of the nation's key problems.

As a result, many think it is necessary to clean up the trust environment: 68 percent say it is very important to repair the public's level of confidence in the federal government, and 58 perent say the same about improving confidence in fellow Americans.

Moreover, some see fading trust as a sign of cultural sickness and national decline. Some also tie it to what they perceive to be increased loneliness and excessive individualism. About half of Americans (49 percent) link the decline in interpersonal trust to a belief that people are not as reliable as they used to be. Many ascribe shrinking trust to a political culture they believe is broken and spawns suspicion, even cynicism, about the ability of others to distinguish fact from fiction.

In a comment typical of the views expressed by many people of different political leanings, ages and educational backgrounds, one participant in a new Pew Research Center survey said: "Many people no longer think the federal government can actually be a force for good or change in their lives. This kind of apathy and disengagement will lead to an even worse and less representative government." Another addressed the issue of fading interpersonal trust: "As a democracy founded on the principle of *E Pluribus Unum*, the fact that we are divided and can't trust sound facts means we have lost our confidence in each other."

Even as they express doleful views about the state of trust today, many Americans believe the situation can be turned around. Fully 84 percent believe the level of confidence Americans have in the federal government can be improved, and 86 percent think improvement is possible when it comes to the confidence Americans have in each other. Among the solutions they offer in their open-ended comments: muffle political partisanship and group-centered tribalism, refocus news coverage away from insult-ridden talk shows and sensationalist stories, stop giving so much attention to digital screens and spend more time with people, and practice empathy. Some believe their neighborhoods are a key place where interpersonal trust can be rebuilt if people work together on local projects, in turn radiating trust out to other sectors of the culture.

The new survey of 10,618 U.S. adults, conducted Nov. 27-Dec. 10, 2018, using the center's nationally representative American Trends Panel, covers a wide range of trust-related issues and adds context to debates about the state of trust and distrust in the nation. The margin of sampling error for the full sample is plus or minus 1.5 percentage points.

In addition to asking traditional questions about whether Americans have confidence in institutions and other human beings, the survey explores links between institutional trust and interpersonal trust and examines the degree to which the public thinks the nation is shackled by these issues. This research is part of the center's extensive and ongoing focus on issues tied to trust, facts and democracy and the interplay among them.

Here are some of the main findings.

There are some partisan differences, too, when it comes to confidence in Americans to act in some civically beneficial ways. For instance, 76 percent of Republicans and 63 percent of Democrats (including independents who lean toward each party) have confidence people would do what they can to help those in need. Similarly, 56 percent of Republicans and 42 percent of Democrats have confidence the American people respect the rights of people who are not like them.

Partisan differences also show up in the levels of trust extended toward various kinds of leaders, including the military, religious leaders and business leaders (groups toward whom Republicans are more favorable than Democrats) as well as scientists, public school principals, college professors, and journalists (groups that generally enjoy more confidence among Democrats than among Republicans).

There is a generation gap in levels of trust

Young adults are much more pessimistic than older adults about some trust issues. For example, young adults are about half as hopeful as their elders when they are asked how confident they are in the American people to respect the rights of those who are not like them: About one-third (35 percent) of those ages 18 to 29 are confident Americans have that respect, compared with two-thirds (67 percent) of those 65 and older.

There is also a gap when it comes to confidence that Americans will do what they can to help others in need. More than four-in-ten young adults (44 percent) are confident the American people will accept election results no matter who wins, compared with 66 percent of older adults who believe that's the case.

At the same time, older Americans are more likely to believe Americans have lost confidence in each other because people are not as reliable as they used to be: 54 percent of those ages 65 and older take this position, compared with 44 percent of those 18 to 29.

Majorities believe the federal government and news media withhold important and useful information

And notable numbers say they struggle to know what's true or not when listening to elected officials. People's confidence in key institutions is associated with their views about how those institutions handle important information. About two-thirds (69 percent) of Americans say the federal government intentionally withholds important information from the public that it could safely release, and about six in ten (61 percent) say the news media intentionally ignores stories that are important to the public. Those who hold these views that information is being withheld are more likely than others to have greater concerns about the state of trust.

Significant shares also assert they face challenges separating the truth from false information when they are listening to elected officials and using social media. Some 64 percent say it is hard to tell the difference between what is true and not true when they hear elected officials; 48 percent say the same thing about information they encounter on social media.

On a grand scale of national issues, trust-related issues are not near the top of the list of Americans' concerns

But people link distrust to the major problems they see, such as concerns about ethics in government and the role of lobbyists and special interests. The Center has asked questions in multiple surveys about how Americans judge the severity of some key issues. This poll finds that 41% of adults think the public's level of confidence in the federal government is a "very big problem," putting it roughly on par with their assessment of the size of the problems caused by racism and illegal immigration—and above terrorism and sexism. Some 25 percent say Americans' level of confidence in each other is a very big problem, which is low in comparison with a broad array of other issues that Americans perceive as major problems.

It is important to note, though, that some Americans see distrust as a factor inciting or amplifying other issues they consider crucial. For example, in their open-ended written answers to questions, numbers of Americans say they think there are direct connections between rising distrust and other trends they perceived as major problems, such as partisan paralysis in government, the outsize influence of lobbyists and moneyed interests, confusion arising from made-up news and information, declining ethics in government, the intractability of immigration and climate debates, rising health-care costs and a widening gap between the rich and the poor.

Many of the answers in the open-ended written responses reflect judgments similar to this one from a 38-year-old man: "Trust is the glue that binds humans together. Without it, we cooperate with one another less, and variables in our overall quality of life are affected (e.g., health and life satisfaction)."

[…]

Notes

1. Our classification of these different groups is explained more fully in Chapter 2 (https://www.pewresearch.org/politics/2019/07/22/the-state-of-personal-trust/#continuum).
2. This survey asked two questions related to public school leaders: one about the public's confidence in principals and superintendents for K-12 schools, the other just about principals (not referencing superintendents). Some 77% of respondents say they have a great deal/fair amount of confidence in public school principals and superintendents. The findings cited throughout this report are from the question focused only on principals.
3. This survey asked two questions related to journalism: one about the public's confidence in journalists, the other about confidence in "the news media." Some 48% of respondents say they have a great deal/fair amount of confidence in the news media. The findings cited throughout this report are from the question about journalists.

VIEWPOINT 2

> "It is clear that untruths about the intentions and beliefs of political parties may be undermining our democracy."

Diagnosing and Addressing Polarized Psychology Can Help Fight Polarization
Beyond Conflict

According to a report by the organization Beyond Conflict, toxic levels of polarization are a major threat to American democracy today. However, their findings also indicate that Republicans overestimate how much Democrats dehumanize, dislike, and disagree with them, and Democrats overestimate the extent to which Republicans do the same. These misunderstandings lead to higher levels of political polarization and animosity than are necessary. By communicating more clearly about the intentions and beliefs of each political party and finding common ground, it may be possible to combat polarization. Beyond Conflict is a Boston-based organization that provides programs and research on global conflict resolution.

As you read, consider the following questions:

1. According to the data collected by Beyond Conflict, what is the difference between the dehumanization score

"Understanding the Psychology That Drives Us Apart," Beyond Conflict. Reprinted by permission.

Republicans think Democrats give them and the score they actually give them?
2. What are the three divides explored in this viewpoint?
3. How does perceived disagreement on gun control compare to reality, according to this viewpoint?

Deepening toxic polarization in the United States is a profound threat to the American people and to the very core of American democracy. After 30 years of working around the globe to bring peace and reconciliation to deeply divided societies, Beyond Conflict launched an unprecedented research project in 2018, the Beyond Conflict Polarization Index™, with leading brain and behavioral scientists to assess the psychological factors that fuel polarization. Our goal is to use psychological insights to develop strategies that enable individuals, institutions, and leaders to address the increasing threat of toxic polarization.

Our research has found a consistent pattern. There is a wide divide between perception and reality across key measures of the Beyond Conflict Polarization Index™. Americans incorrectly believe that members of the other party dehumanize, dislike, and disagree with them about twice as much as they actually do. In short, we believe we're more polarized than we really are—and that misperception can drive us even further apart. The divide is correlated with outcomes that are consequential for democracy and represent a new degree of toxic polarization in America.

When it's fully built, the Polarization Index will be used as a diagnostic tool and source of reference for organizations (e.g. journalists, politicians, civic organizations, advocacy groups, religious and other local and national organizations) looking to determine if they are increasing or decreasing polarization.

#1 The Dehumanization Divide: Republicans and Democrats believe that members of the other party dehumanize them more than twice as much as they actually do

Dehumanization is the act of seeing other people as less than human. It is a dangerous psychological process and a strong indicator of potential hostility between groups.

Levels of dehumanization between Republicans and Democrats are concerning. But what's even more concerning are the levels of perceived dehumanization–the degree to which we feel dehumanized by members of an opposing group. Republicans and Democrats believe that members of the other party dehumanize them more than twice as much as they actually do. Specifically, Republicans estimate that Democrats rate them a score of 28 out of 100 (in reality Democrats rated them at an 83). Similarly, Democrats estimate that Republicans rate them 48 points out of 100 (in reality Republicans rated them at an 80).

#2 The Dislike Divide: Republicans and Democrats overestimate how much the other party dislikes them

The most common feature of polarized psychology is strong feelings of dislike toward members of the other party. Current levels of dislike are strong and widespread: When asked how cold (0) or warm (100) they feel about the other party, Republicans give Democrats a score of approximately 34 out of 100, while Democrats give Republicans a score of 28 out of 100.

Yet as strong as dislike it, Americans believe it is substantially greater than it is. Democrats believe Republicans' feelings of dislike toward them are 17 points lower than they really are, while Republicans believe that Democrats' feelings toward them are 13 points lower than they really are. Overestimating how much the other party dislikes your party is predictive of higher levels of social distance (e.g., feeling uncomfortable with members of the other party serving as your doctor, being your child's teacher, or marrying one of your children).

#3 The Disagreement Divide: Republicans and Democrats overestimate the extent of partisan disagreement on key issues

Americans also exaggerate the extent of partisan disagreement on policy issues. We asked members of each party to rate their own views on immigration. We did not ask about specific policies, but rather about general preference for closed or open borders, noting that many people are not in either extreme. In our survey, 0 means keeping all borders completely open to all migrants and 100 means keeping all borders completely closed to all migrants. We also asked them to estimate how the average member of the other party would answer the same question.

In our samples, Democrats had a median score of 35, but Republicans estimated that Democrats would have a median score of 9. Meanwhile, Republicans had a median score of 75, while Democrats estimated Republicans would have a median score of 92.

We created a similar measurement scale for gun control. In our survey, 0 means repealing the Second Amendment and outlawing guns, and 100 means enforcing no restrictions on gun ownership. We also asked respondents to rate how they think the average Republican or the average Democrat would answer the same question about gun control.

Members of both parties believe the extent of disagreement on gun control is greater than in reality. Republicans estimated that Democrats would place themselves at 11. In reality, Democrats placed themselves at a median score of 35. Meanwhile, Democrats estimated that Republicans would be at a median score of 94, while Republicans placed themselves at a median score of 74.

Future Directions for the Polarization Index

America faces profound challenges that are largely unaddressed, partly due to rising sentiments of mutual animosity between Democrats and Republicans. Our research indicates that the country is not as divided as it seems and that Americans are ideologically closer to one another than they believe. It is clear that untruths about the intentions and beliefs of political parties may be undermining our democracy.

In order to effectively address toxic polarization, we must develop the ability to diagnose, understand, and address the dynamics of a polarized psychology. We need to measure the degree of toxic polarization to combat it. The Beyond Conflict Polarization Index™ systematically tracks polarized psychology and produces actionable insights that citizens, opinion leaders, and civic organizations can translate into programs and action. An evidence-based understanding of the psychology of partisan animosity among the public offers an opportunity to take action in the lead-up to the 2020 elections and beyond.

VIEWPOINT 3

> "Treating friendship as a prerequisite to cooperation also misses the fact that people have long worked together for the common good on the basis of relationships that do not resemble the intimacy of friends."

Bridging the Political Divide Requires Tolerance and Cooperation, Not Friendship

Francesca Polletta

Many have argued that promoting conversation between people of opposing political parties and increasing feelings of intimacy and friendship between these groups would help decrease political polarization and animosity. However, this viewpoint by Francesca Polletta argues that this may not necessarily be the case. Through examining political polarization workshops, Polletta found that the exchanges that were most effective were when participants challenged and voiced their opposition toward certain beliefs, not when they tried to find commonalities. Polletta asserts that empathy and friendship is unnecessary in bridging the political divide, but that showing tolerance toward others and a willingness to cooperate with them is more effective. Francesca Polletta is a professor of sociology at the University of California, Irvine.

"Bridging America's Divides Requires a Willingness to Work Together Without Becoming Friends First," by Francesca Polletta, The Conversation, October 9, 2020. https://theconversation.com/bridging-americas-divides-requires-a-willingness-to-work-together-without-becoming-friends-first-143648. Licensed under CC BY-4.0 International.

As you read, consider the following questions:

1. When did Joan Blades launch Living Room Conversations?
2. According to researchers cited in this viewpoint, what conditions make initiatives to bring people of different groups together less effective?
3. According to research from the University of Houston mentioned in this viewpoint, how are people who are naturally empathetic more likely to feel toward members of the opposing party?

Amid two crises—the pandemic and the national reckoning sparked by the killing of George Floyd—there have been anguished calls for Americans to come together across lines of race and partisanship. Change would come, a *USA Today* contributor wrote, only "when we become sensitized to the distress of our neighbors."

Empathy born of intimacy was the prepandemic solution to the nation's fractured political landscape. If Americans could simply get to know one another, to share stories and appreciate each other's struggles, civic leaders argued, we would develop a sense of understanding and empathy that would extend beyond the single encounter.

But after studying how Americans cooperate, both in moments of political upheaval and in ordinary times, I am convinced that tackling America's political divide demands more than intimacy— and less than it.

Ordinary People, Talking

Science bears out the idea that intimacy can make people more understanding of others.

A venerable tradition of social psychological research shows that people who interact with members of a stigmatized group may change their opinion of the whole group. The original research by Gordon Allport suggested that contact between members of different groups worked by giving people knowledge of the other group. But later studies found instead that it increased their empathy and willingness to take the other's perspective.

That's why a growing industry of professional facilitators champion carefully structured conversations as key to solving workplace conflicts, community development disputes, Americans' political disengagement and racial division.

As partisan political divides became vitriolic, civic leaders brought ordinary people together to talk. You could join people from the left and right at a Make America Dinner Again event or a Better Angels workshop, where "you can actually become friends and colleagues with people you don't agree with."

Joan Blades, who created the online political advocacy group MoveOn.Org in 1997, seemed to have her finger on the pulse again when she launched Living Room Conversations in 2011. Small groups would host conversations across partisan lines.

"By the time you get to the topic you've chosen to discuss, you're thinking, 'I like this person or these people,'" Blades promised.

By the end of the 2010s, these were the terms for building unity: personal conversations in intimate settings that would produce friendship across gulfs of difference.

Commonalities and Differences

The pandemic made the idea of living room conversations with anyone outside one's household sadly unrealistic. But it may not have been the solution people were looking for in the first place.

Initiatives that bring together members of different groups, researchers have shown, are less effective in reducing prejudice when the groups participating are unequal in power and status—say, Black Americans and white ones.

Dominant group members tend to insist on talking about their commonalities with members of the disadvantaged group. That's frustrating for the latter, who more often want to talk about their differences and, indeed, their inequalities.

Taking the perspective of someone different, moreover, works to diminish the prejudices of members of dominant groups but not those of members of disadvantaged groups. Research also shows that when people are asked to take the perspective of a person who fits a stereotype, they negatively stereotype that person even more than if they had not been asked to do so. Asking a Democrat to put herself in the shoes of a MAGA hat-wearing Republican, in other words, may backfire.

Nor does empathy always overcome political beliefs.

A recent study from the University of Houston found that people who are naturally empathetic are more likely to feel anger toward those in the opposite party and feel pleasure when they suffer. Empathy tends to be biased toward one's own group, so it may fuel political polarization rather than counter it.

Naturally empathetic people are also more likely to suppress their feelings of compassion when those feelings conflict with their ideological views, becoming less compassionate as a result. In one study, subjects who had individualistic beliefs opposed government welfare programs even after reading a story about a man in financial need, but individualists who were naturally empathetic opposed welfare even more strongly after reading the story.

Friendship Isn't Necessary

Since dialogue initiatives are voluntary, they probably attract people who are already predisposed to wanting to find connection across difference. And no one has figured out how a friendly meeting between Democratic and Republican voters, or even a hundred such meetings, can have a discernible effect on political polarization that is national in scope.

Certainly, participants who change their minds may share their new opinions with others in their circle, creating a ripple effect of goodwill. But dialogue initiatives may also crowd out ways of tackling political divisions that are likely to have wider impact.

Americans committed to living in a functioning democracy could demand that national political representatives, not ordinary

VIEWPOINT 4

| *"With a Democratic-Republican duopoly controlling the levers of government, we can hardly say this is a democratic system of government."*

Getting Rid of the Two-Party System Could Help America Overcome Its Divide

David A. Love

In this viewpoint, David A. Love argues that the two-party system is not an essential part of America's political structure, and that in fact it has a damaging impact on American democracy. Because there is no viable alternative to the Republican and Democratic parties in the form of a third party, things like cooperating on legislation and maintaining strong approval ratings are not a strong priority, which leads to greater political dysfunction and polarization. Introducing strong alternatives to these two parties would encourage politicians to be more effective and act in the interest of their constituents. David A. Love is a journalist and commentator who writes investigative stories and op-eds on a variety of issues.

As you read, consider the following questions:

1. According to this viewpoint, are political parties addressed in the U.S. Constitution?

"It's Time to Get Rid of the Two-Party System," by David A. Love, WHYY, INC., April 14, 2017. Reprinted by permission.

2. At the time this viewpoint was published in 2017, how many states had voter ID laws?
3. How much money did Democrats spend on the 2016 election, according to this viewpoint?

Now is the time for us to consider scrapping the two-party system of government. Now is about the best time to reflect on how our politics has failed to serve the public, and to begin to replace it.

The U.S. Constitution does not mention political parties, much less require two of them. On the surface, there is nothing inherently wrong with political parties. The problem is when these parties assume too much power and suck all the air out of the room that is American democracy. With a Democratic-Republican duopoly controlling the levers of government, we can hardly say this is a democratic system of government.

Entrenched power has resulted in the corrupting influence of money in politics, something which has impacted both major parties. The U.S. Supreme Court's Citizens United decision ushered in the era of unlimited corporate money in political campaigns—anonymous, unaccountable, and overwhelming in influence. With corporations acting as citizens, and campaign donations as a form of free speech, what chance can ordinary citizens have to make their voices heard?

When the elected officials and their parties receive their funding from one source and their votes from another, the funders will win. And the result is a system of legalized bribery in which politicians are beholden to financial interests—so-called dark money—perhaps even flowing from foreign nations.

The partisan and racial gerrymandering of districts—which currently disproportionately benefits the Republican Party—has created one-party rule in some parts of the country, allowing politicians to select their own constituents, rather than the other way around. Redistricting does not encourage moderate,

> ## More Political Parties Would Improve American Democracy
>
> The massive divide our nation is experiencing provides a compelling reason to reevaluate the American election process. Making structural changes to our system could address many underlying causes of this division and ultimately unite Americans.
>
> For years, voters have expressed their desire to cast their vote for someone outside of the binary choice they have been given, but they fear that a vote for a third party will be wasted, or worse, unintentionally result in the election of the establishment party candidate they like least.
>
> George Washington's farewell address is often remembered for its warning against hyper-partisanship: "The alternate domination of one faction over another, sharpened by the spirit of revenge, natural to party dissension, which in different ages and countries has perpetrated the most horrid enormities, is itself a frightful despotism."

heterogeneous districts, but rather can provide a particular political party with a majority of seats in a state legislature or a state congressional delegation, a potentially insurmountable advantage for the opposing party to overcome. Racial gerrymandering also dilutes the power of voters of color and renders them invisible.

The Republicans have enacted voter suppression measures in the state houses they control throughout the country. Such laws, which include voter ID (34 states in all), are designed to disenfranchise Blacks people, Latinos, and other traditionally non-Republican constituencies. Now, Republicans in at least 10 states have proposed legislation to criminalize peaceful political protest.

On the national level, the two major parties are at risk of imploding or atrophying. Due to their dysfunction, the government is ill-equipped to solve America's myriad problems—climate

> John Adams, Washington's successor, similarly worried that "a division of the republic into two great parties ... is to be dreaded as the great political evil."
>
> Americans should welcome the departure of the two-party system and instead encourage members of either political party who feel disenfranchised to create new political parties that better fit their ideologies and beliefs. Watching cable news, you'll see views on the far ends of the political spectrum, but the majority of Americans are centrist and simply want the government to effectively provide core services.
>
> Most importantly, rather than continuing to force the square peg of their political beliefs into the round hole of Republican or Democrat, voters would finally have the opportunity to support a party with which they truly identify. As many aspiring presidential candidates have learned, attempting to force an established political party to morph to fit one's belief is an exercise in futility.
>
> "We Need to Get Rid of the Two-Party System," by Lyle Larson, Galveston Newspapers, June 9, 2020.

change, poverty, gun violence, unemployment, and student loans. Democrats spent over $1 billion in the 2016 election with little to show for it, a culmination of years of tone deafness, and eschewing their labor union base in favor of neoliberal policies promoted by their corporate donors.

Under President Donald Trump, the Republicans have become a party of extremism, of unabashed white nationalism, Muslim bans, and border walls. Both Congress and the president have low approval ratings, and the executive branch is in a crisis that screams for substantive reform. The Trump administration is engaged in the wholesale dismantling of government agencies. A kleptocratic cabinet of billionaires has a combined net worth greater than one-third of the U.S. population. The president hires his family like a banana republic dictator, and he uses his position to profit from his businesses. Allegations of Russian collusion in the 2016 election notwithstanding, these are all symptoms of a larger disease plaguing the American body politic.

American politics discourages the development of viable third parties, a rigged system that renders these independent efforts little more than a protest vote. If democracy is to thrive in the U.S., we need new voices and a range of points of view to flourish. More democratic participation and civic engagement is the antidote. This includes replacing our winner-take-all electoral scheme with multi-seat congressional districts or a parliamentary-type system of proportional representation in which political parties would receive seats in the legislature in proportion to the votes they receive.

A multi-party arrangement would encourage coalition-building and compromise, rather than the pathological gridlock that characterizes American government. This will only work by lifting of all barriers to voting, removing big money from elections, and encouraging more people to go to the polls and run for office. There's nothing to lose, and the only alternative is to continue to suffer through the national embarrassment that passes for the U.S. political system.

VIEWPOINT 5

> "The two-party system will survive, regardless of political turbulence. This is a result of how the U.S. elects leaders."

The Two-Party System Is an Essential Part of American Democracy

Alexander Cohen

In the following viewpoint Alexander Cohen explains that despite the fact that the majority of Americans are dissatisfied with the two-party system and would like a third political party, this is highly unlikely to happen. This is because having political parties simplifies the electoral process, and adding more political parties would make it more complicated. The reason political parties have failed in national politics in America is because voters do not want to waste their vote on a candidate that is unlikely to be elected. The two main parties try to appeal to a wide coalition of voters, so voters can generally choose one that they identify with more closely to vote for. Alexander Cohen is an assistant professor of political science at Clarkson University.

As you read, consider the following questions:

1. According to data cited in this viewpoint, what percent of Americans think a third political party is necessary?

"The Two-Party System Is Here to Stay," by Alexander Cohen, The Conversation, March 2, 2020. https://theconversation.com/the-two-party-system-is-here-to-stay-132423. Licensed under CC BY 4.0 International.

When the question of federal supremacy was settled, the Anti-Federalists were replaced by the Democratic-Republican Party, which championed Southern agricultural interests. When the Federalists died out, the Democratic-Republican Party split into the Whigs and Democrats, who disagreed about the balance of power between branches of government.

By 1856, a collapsing Whig Party was replaced by the anti-slavery Republican Party, whose feuds with the pro-slavery Democrats led to the Civil War.

From that point forward, those two dominant national parties have remained stable. Third-party challenges have been limited and generally unimportant, usually driven by specific issues rather than broad-based concerns.

Stability in the Future

The modern Republicans and Democrats are unlikely to go the way of the Whigs, Federalists, and Anti-Federalists, regardless of recent political earthquakes.

National politics are a different game now than they were during the early republic. Advances in communication and technology have enhanced party organization. Parties can maintain a truly national presence and ward off potential challengers. Both major parties have shown a willingness to stretch to accommodate populists like Trump and Sanders rather than splintering.

Recent changes in the Democratic nomination process, for example, demonstrate this flexibility. Barriers to third parties appearing on ballots are ingrained in our electoral laws, which have been engineered by those managing the current system so that it will endure.

And donors and lobbyists, who want predictable outcomes, have little incentive to rock the boat by supporting a new player in the game.

Certainly, the parties have evolved and will continue to do so. For example, the once reliably Democratic "solid South" shifted to Republican control beginning with the civil rights movement. Yet evolution should not be confused with destruction, and the persistence of the present system is relatively secure.

Periodical and Internet Sources Bibliography

The following articles have been selected to supplement the diverse views presented in this chapter.

John Burnett, "Red/Blue Workshops Try to Bridge Divide. Do They Really Work?" NPR, April 6, 2022. https://www.npr.org/2022/04/06/1090910863/red-blue-workshops-try-to-bridge-the-political-divide-do-they-really-work.

Lee Drutman, "The Two-Party System Is Killing Our Democracy," *Vox,* January 23, 2020. https://www.vox.com/2020/1/23/21075960/polarization-parties-ranked-choice-voting-proportional-representation.

Jacob Hess, "Perspective: The Braver Angels Plan to Heal America," *Deseret News*, March 10, 2022. https://www.deseret.com/2022/3/9/22949616/perspective-the-braver-angels-miracle-polarization-democrats-republicans-dialogue-politics-election.

Tammy Joyner, "What Will It Take to Shake Up America's Two-Party Political System?" *Atlanta Civic Circle*, March 15, 2022. https://atlantaciviccircle.org/2022/03/15/what-will-it-take-to-shake-up-americas-two-party-political-system/.

Rachel Kleinfeld and Aaron Sobel, "7 Ideas to Reduce Polarization. And Save America from Itself," *USA Today*, July 23, 2020. https://www.usatoday.com/story/opinion/2020/07/23/political-polarization-dangerous-america-heres-how-fight-column/5477711002/.

Danielle Kurtzlebaum, "What If We Don't Need to 'Fix' Polarization?" NPR, March 26, 2021. https://www.npr.org/2021/03/19/979369761/is-todays-bitter-partisanship-a-step-toward-a-more-equal-democracy.

Michael W. Macy, Manqing Ma, Daniel R. Tabin, and Boleslaw K. Szymanski, "Polarization and Tipping Points," *Proceedings of the National Academy of Sciences*, December 6, 2021. https://www.pnas.org/doi/10.1073/pnas.2102144118.

Erik Santoro and David E. Broockman, "The Promise and Pitfalls of Cross-Partisan Conversations for Reducing Affective Polarization: Evidence from Randomized Experiments," *Science*

Advances, June 22, 2022. https://www.science.org/doi/10.1126/sciadv.abn5515.

Nathan Stock, "How to Reduce Political Violence in America," openDemocracy, August 18, 2020. https://www.opendemocracy.net/en/transformation/how-reduce-political-violence-america/.

Robert B. Talisse, "Civility in Politics Is Harder than You Think," the *Conversation*, February 5, 2020. https://theconversation.com/civility-in-politics-is-harder-than-you-think-130522.

For Further Discussion

Chapter 1
1. Does the viewpoint by Anne N. Junod, Clare Salerno, and Corianne Payton Scally about the urban-rural divide necessarily contradict the viewpoint on this topic by Alexandra Kanik and Patrick Scott? Explain your answer.
2. Do you find Christos A. Makridis' argument that income equality is more likely to be the cause of polarization, rather than the other way around, convincing? Why or why not?
3. How does the data in the viewpoint by Michael Dimock and Richard Wike support or contradict claims in other viewpoints from this chapter?

Chapter 2
1. How much responsibility do you think the media bears for a divided America?
2. What do the viewpoints in this chapter suggest are some of the causes of increasing polarization and division in American politics? Which of the potential causes do you find most persuasive?
3. In the viewpoint by Naomi Schalit and Ore Koren, Koren asserts that a strong response by the government against acts of political violence can help prevent more political violence in the future. What kinds of responses by the government do you think are necessary after acts of political violence?

Chapter 3
1. What are some of the reasons why the U.S. seems to be polarizing faster than other democracies around the world mentioned in the viewpoints in this chapter?
2. Do you find Ken Stern's argument that the American public is not as divided as politicians want them to believe

convincing? Why or why not? Use data or examples provided in the viewpoints from this chapter to support your answer.
3. According to the viewpoints in this chapter, what does it mean to be restrictionist? What are some examples of restrictionist attitudes or policies presented in these viewpoints?

Chapter 4

1. Compare the data presented in the viewpoint by Lee Rainie, Scott Keeter, and Andrew Perrin from the Pew Research Center and the data in the viewpoint from Beyond Conflict. How does the data in one viewpoint support or contradict the findings of the other viewpoint?
2. Francesca Polletta argues that empathy and friendship between people from different political and sociological backgrounds are not necessary for cooperation between these groups. Do you agree or disagree? Explain your answer.
3. Why does Alexander Cohen assert that the U.S. will continue to have a two-party political system? Do you agree with his reasoning? Why or why not?

Organizations to Contact

The editors have compiled the following list of organizations concerned with the issues debated in this book. The descriptions are derived from materials provided by the organizations. All have publications or information available for interested readers. The list was compiled on the date of publication of the present volume; the information provided here may change. Be aware that many organizations take several weeks or longer to respond to inquiries, so allow as much time as possible.

American Civil Liberties Union (ACLU)

125 Broad Street, 18th Floor
New York, NY 10004
(212) 549-2500
website: www.aclu.org

The American Civil Liberties Union (ACLU) is a nonprofit organization that was founded in 1920 with the intention of defending the individual rights and liberties guaranteed by the Constitution, including the right to vote. It has filed numerous lawsuits across the U.S. to help secure and protect voting rights. It also launched the "Let People Vote" campaign to inform the public on their voting rights, provide them information on how to vote by mail, and keep them updated on important election deadlines.

Braver Angels

733 Third Avenue, 16th Floor
New York, NY 10170
(212) 246-3942
email: info@braverangels.org
website: braverangels.org

Braver Angels is a nonprofit citizens' organization that is focused on depolarizing American politics. It facilitates online debates, online and in-person workshops, documentary screenings, and one-on-one conversations for Americans across the political spectrum to promote greater understanding. Its website also includes a library of resources to help bridge the political divide.

Bridge Alliance

1370 Haymaker Rd.
State College, PA 16801
(202) 875-7531
email: info@BridgeAlliance.us
website: www.bridgealliance.us

Bridge Alliance is a nonprofit coalition of over 100 member organizations. Its mission is to bridge the partisan political divide and to transform American politics to allow for greater self-governance. Its member organizations work on civic engagement, campaigns and electoral processes, and governance and policymaking.

The Heritage Foundation

214 Massachusetts Ave. NE
Washington DC, 20002
(202) 546-4400
email: info@heritage.org
website: www.heritage.org

The Heritage Foundation is a conservative American think tank that is geared toward public policy. Its website features articles on wide range of issues impacting the U.S., including culture, poverty, and politics. The foundation aims to put power back into the hands of the American public by not working on behalf of special interest groups or political parties.

National Association of Nonpartisan Reformers (NANR)

1580 Lincoln Street, Suite 520
Denver, CO 80203
email: contact@nonpartisanreformers.org
website: nonpartisanreformers.org

The National Association of Nonpartisan Reformers is a member-led association that is dedicated to making structural election reforms that benefit the public interest. Though not opposed to political parties, the organization supports campaigns that increase electoral competition. They support the increased participation of numerous political parties and independents in politics.

Rural Assembly

46 E. Main Street
Whitesburg, KY 41858
(865) 688-9546
email: tracy@ruralstrategies.org
website: ruralassembly.org

Rural Assembly is an organization that aims to reframe how the media, politicians, and the public understand rural America. It aims to challenge stereotypes that dominate public discourse on rural America while addressing the health, economic, and social issues that impact Americans in rural areas. The organization runs campaigns and events to promote greater understanding of rural America.

Urban Institute

500 L'Enfant Plaza SW
Washington, DC 20024
(202) 833-7200
website: www.urban.org

The Urban Institute is a nonprofit research institute that aims to provide data and evidence to policymakers and the public about the issues that affect urban America. The organization helps foundations, philanthropists, journalists, and members of the public understand the research and gain a better understanding of urban America and how to address the issues faced by people in these areas. Its website includes stories, data tools, and blogs on these topics.

Bibliography of Books

Thomas Carothers and Andrew O'Donohue, eds. *Democracies Divided: The Global Challenge of Political Polarization*. Washington, DC: Brookings Institution Press, 2019.

Curtis Chesney. *Roots of Division: Uncovering What Lies Beneath America's Racial Divide*. Greensboro, NC: Rooted Press, 2020.

David F. Damore, Robert E. Lang, and Karen A Danielsen. *Blue Metros, Red States: The Shifting Urban-Rural Divide in America's Swing States*. Washington, DC: Brookings Institution Press, 2020.

Andrew Hartman. *A War for the Soul of America: A History of the Culture Wars*. 2nd ed. Chicago, IL: University of Chicago Press, 2019.

Bridey Heing, ed. *America's Urban-Rural Divide* (Introducing Issues with Opposing Viewpoints). New York, NY: Greenhaven Publishing, 2019.

Avery Elizabeth Hurt, ed. *Party Politics* (Opposing Viewpoints). New York, NY: Greenhaven Publishing, 2020.

Richard Kreitner. *Break It Up: Secession, Division, and the Secret History of America's Imperfect Union*. New York, NY: Little, Brown and Company, 2020.

Yanna Krupnikov and John Barry Ryan. *The Other Divide: Polarization and Disengagement in American Politics*. Cambridge, UK: Cambridge University Press, 2022.

Stephen Marche. *The Next Civil War: Dispatches from the American Future*. New York, NY: Avid Reader Press, 2022.

Carla Mooney, ed. *Partisanship* (At Issue). New York, NY: Greenhaven Publishing, 2021.

Adam M. Silver. *Partisanship and Polarization: American Party Platforms, 1840–1896*. Lanham, MD: Lexington Books, 2022.

Margaret Sullivan. *Ghosting the News: Local Journalism and the Crisis of American Democracy*. New York, NY: Columbia Global Reports, 2020.

Matt Taibbi. *Hate Inc.: Why the Media Makes Us Despise One Another*. New York, NY: OR Books, 2019.

Gary Wiener, ed. *The Capitol Riot: Fragile Democracy* (Current Controversies). New York, NY: Greenhaven Publishing, 2022.

Index

A
Australia, 107–108

B
Bangladesh, 104, 111, 114, 116
Biden, Joe, 21, 24–26, 47–50, 65
Black Lives Matter, 51, 56, 80, 83
Black Americans, 18, 31, 43–44, 51–59, 136, 150, 152
Bolsonaro, Jair, 113
Brazil, 104, 110–113
Brexit, 47, 104, 114, 117–118
Bush, George H. W., 70
Bush, George W., 69

C
Canada, 107–108
Capitol building attack, U.S., 14, 65, 83, 88–93
Carter, Jimmy, 69
Chávez, Hugo, 113
Clinton, Bill, 70
Clinton, Hillary, 21, 31, 39, 81
Colombia, 104, 111–112
COVID-19 pandemic, 46–49, 91, 149–151

E
Ecuador, 115
education, 14, 18–19, 30, 32, 65, 136

Electoral College, 24, 26
Erdoğan, Recep Tayyip, 112

F
Ford, Gerald, 69
France, 104, 118–121

G
gender, 51–54, 58, 60
Germany, 107–108, 118–121
gerrymandering, 74–77, 156

H
Hungary, 104

I
identity politics, 41–42, 51–61
immigration, 16, 32, 141–142, 146
India, 104, 110–113, 115
Indonesia, 104, 111
Italy, 104

K
Kaczyński, Jarosław, 112
Kenya, 104, 111–112, 115

L
Lincoln, Abraham, 124

M

Malaysia, 104
Modi, Narendra, 112
Moreno, Lenín, 115

N

New Zealand, 107–108
Nixon, 92
Norway, 107–108

O

Obama, Barack, 42, 70
Occupy Wall Street, 72–73

P

Poland, 104, 110–113
political parties
  Anti-Federalists, 14, 161–162
  Democratic-Republicans, 162
  Democrats, 14–17, 20–21, 23–26, 36, 38, 40–48, 57, 69–73, 80–82, 94–96, 98, 100, 107–108, 118, 123, 125–127, 136, 139–140, 144–147, 151, 155–162
  Federalists, 14, 161–162
  Republicans, 14–17, 20–21, 24, 26, 36, 38, 41–48, 69–72, 74, 80–82, 94–96, 98, 100, 107–108, 118, 121, 126–127, 139–140, 144–147, 151, 155–162
  Whigs, 162

R

race, 14–15, 18–19, 31, 40–47, 49, 51–60, 73, 76, 104, 108, 136, 149–152
Reagan, Ronald, 59, 69–70, 92
religion, 14–15, 17, 41, 43–46, 49, 104, 108, 114, 116, 118–121, 123

S

Sanders, Bernie, 39, 73, 160, 162
social media, 48, 81, 84–85, 96–98, 98, 112, 141
Sri Lanka, 104
Sweden, 104, 107–108
Switzerland, 107–108

T

Tea Party, 72–73, 128
Trump, Donald, 20–26, 29, 31, 45, 47–49, 59, 81, 83–84, 87, 93–94, 99, 118, 121, 127, 157, 160, 162
Turkey, 111–115
two-party system, 14–15, 46, 48, 65, 68, 80–85, 88, 131–132, 154–158

U

United Kingdom, 104, 107–109, 114, 117–121
urban-rural divide, 16–17, 20–26, 28–33

… Index

V
Venezuela, 112

W
Washington, George, 82, 156–157, 160